C000246219

Olivia Petter is a journalist a
She has written for the *Sun
Refinery29* and the *Independ
relationships writer and host of its chart-topping *Millennial Love* podcast. This is her first book.

Praise for *Millennial Love*:

'*Millennial Love* is easy to read and Petter is an engaging guide to sensitive, personal subjects. The author is also remarkably candid about her own insecurities and mistakes, and brave enough to detail some of her own harrowing experiences. Hopefully, this honest, important book will leave a lot of young readers feeling more reassured and better informed about their own lives' ***INDEPENDENT*** **(an *Independent* Book of the Year)**

'An insightful, honest guide to the vagaries of modern love' **ELIZABETH DAY**

'A mouthpiece for our anxieties and a tonic for our hearts, Petter perfectly dissects why we're not insane when it comes to love, the realities are their own madness' **CHARLY COX**

'Funny and honest' **PANDORA SYKES**

'Olivia Petter is a great journalist and a sharp-eyed chronicler of modern life, and offers readers of all stripes and ages a great overview of relationships in the digital era' **MATT HAIG**

'This is a sharp, funny and reassuring memoir-cum-chronicle of the modern dating landscape, charting everything from the trope of "the cool girl" to the tribulations of contraception in a voice that melds journalistic scrutiny with commendable frankness. Petter's is a world in which Sylvia Plath, *Love Island*, Pandora Sykes and *How to Lose a Guy in 10 Days* collide with satisfying verve...' *VANITY FAIR*

'Honest, hilarious and heart-breaking' *MAIL PLUS*

'Olivia Petter archly discusses and deconstructs the trials and tribulations of dating today with the help of former podcast guests including Munroe Bergdorf and Elizabeth Day, to brilliant effect' *BURO.*

'Entertaining me endlessly' **DAISY LOWE**

'Witty and truthful' **CAGGIE DUNLOP**

'An important read for anyone dating in the time of dating apps' **AJA BARBER**

Millennial Love

Olivia Petter

4th ESTATE · London

4th Estate
An imprint of HarperCollins*Publishers*
1 London Bridge Street
London SE1 9GF

www.4thEstate.co.uk

HarperCollins*Publishers*
1st Floor, Watermarque Building, Ringsend Road
Dublin 4, Ireland

First published in Great Britain in 2021 by 4th Estate
This 4th Estate paperback edition published in 2022

1

Copyright © Olivia Petter 2021

Olivia Petter asserts the moral right to be identified as the author of this
work in accordance with the Copyright, Designs and Patents Act 1988

A catalogue record for this book is available from the British Library

ISBN 978-0-00-841234-0

Extract from 'Mad Girl's Love Song' from *The Bell Jar* by Sylvia Plath
used with permission from Faber and Faber Ltd.

All rights reserved. No part of this publication may be reproduced,
stored in a retrieval system, or transmitted, in any form or by any means,
electronic, mechanical, photocopying, recording or otherwise, without the
prior permission of the publishers.

This book is sold subject to the condition that it shall not, by way of trade
or otherwise, be lent, re-sold, hired out or otherwise circulated without the
publisher's prior consent in any form of binding or cover other than that in
which it is published and without a similar condition including this
condition being imposed on the subsequent purchaser.

Set in Adobe Garamond Pro by Palimpsest Book Production Limited,
Falkirk, Stirlingshire

Printed and Bound in the UK using
100% Renewable Electricity at CPI Group (UK) Ltd

MIX
Paper from
responsible sources
FSC **FSC C007454**

This book is produced from independently certified FSC™ paper
to ensure responsible forest management.

For more information visit: www.harpercollins.co.uk/green

For Coco, the love of my life
(who doesn't like it when I call her 'mum')

Contents

Introduction

Last August, I found myself wandering around Paris alone, looking for somewhere to eat dinner. I was supposed to be there with my boyfriend to celebrate our two-year anniversary, but we'd broken up ten days earlier. Hubris and the belief that my life was like an episode of *Sex and the City* led me to go ahead with the trip. If I went to Paris, I thought, I could skip the heartache, one cliché at a time. I'd peruse antique bookshops and have erudite conversations about Hemingway with strangers. I'd have an epiphany about the meaning of life standing outside Notre-Dame at midnight. And I'd drink plenty of vintage Merlot on the Seine with my newfound French friends. Slowly, as the weekend progressed, my ex would slide from my memory, and all the pain I'd harboured would magically evaporate into the humid Parisian summer air.

Obviously, none of that happened. Instead, I spent hours scrolling through Hinge, smoked enough cigarettes to give myself swollen glands and Facebook-stalked the woman my ex said he'd gone for a drink with earlier that week. She was pretty. It took me forty-five minutes to find somewhere to eat dinner, because every single place I'd been recommended was either too romantic or too Instagrammable for me to feel comfortable sitting there alone. I also can't speak French, which was unhelpful. All of which led to me sobbing into a bowl of cold ravioli in the worst Italian restaurant in Paris.

I'm not an expert at love – far from it. I'm a hopeless hold-me-and-kiss-me-in-the-rain kind of romantic. I over-analyse everything. I weave entire fantasies about people using the barest of threads. I'm anxious but also avoidant. Sometimes I want to be the kind of woman that dances through life and needs no one. Other times I just want to have someone to stroke my hair and tell me I have the best tits they've ever seen.

This is not a book that will tell you how to fall in or out of love – and it certainly won't tell you how to stay in it. What it will do, though (I hope), is illustrate why all these things are more complicated now than they ever have been. Not just for me and those paddling in my shallow pool of experience as a straight, cisgendered white woman. But for all those voices that have generously shared their thoughts and anecdotes with me on the podcast I host for the *Independent*, *Millennial Love*. It is only through speaking to a rich mix of people spanning sexualities, genders and ethnicities that anyone can hope to make sense of this increasingly labyrinthine dating landscape. It is different for everyone, but it is also, in many ways, the same.

Falling in love is one of those rare things in life that almost everyone does; it's a part of what makes us human. Hence why it is such a fascinating subject to interrogate, particularly now. Ostensibly, dating has never been easier. Thanks to the myriad of apps and websites at your disposal, arranging a date has become akin to ordering a takeaway – only the menu, and the number of orders you can place at once, is never-ending. You can whittle down your preferences to the nth degree. If you don't like one dish, there are hundreds, if not thousands, more options to choose from.

Research suggests that by 2031 more than 50 per cent of couples will have met online.* In many ways, this is a good thing. For those in the LGBT+ community, for example, dating apps can be pivotal in helping people facilitate safe and mutually respectful relationships. By giving users the opportunity to state their gender and their sexuality before speaking to a potential partner, it can eliminate the risk of encountering prejudices, such as homophobia or transphobia, that you may be more likely to encounter in real-life interactions. Similarly, online dating can also make things more straightforward, more generally speaking. When you meet someone you fancy in person, it can be difficult to know if they fancy you too. Dating apps remove that ambiguity, because you can typically only speak to another user if you've already expressed a mutual interest in one another. Easy-peasy. Except it isn't, not even a little bit.

I know plenty of people who've formed happy and healthy relationships after meeting online – I'm sure you do, too. But we know this isn't the full story. If dating really was that simple, and everyone could find love at first swipe, we would all be in happy, healthy relationships. There would be no need for dating apps at all, because no one would be single. Research wouldn't be appearing claiming that millennials have less sex than previous generations, because we'd all be boning like bunnies. And no one would find themselves aggressively pursuing some sort of pseudo-Carrie Bradshaw fantasy in Paris.

Love has always lent itself to gameplay. But digital tech has exacerbated this to the point of parody. Consider the ever-

---

* 'Over 50% of couples will meet online by 2031', eHarmony. Available at: https://www.eharmony.co.uk/dating-advice/online-dating-unplugged/over-50-of-couples-will-meet-online-by-2031

expanding list of so-called dating 'trends' (ghosting, benching, breadcrumbing), which now make up an entire dictionary that serves almost exclusively to validate cruel behaviour online. Gone are the days when you'd just approach someone you fancied on a night out and ask for their number. Now, you might check your happn profile to see if they have the app. Or perhaps you'd catch their name and slide into their DMs later that night. Or you'd find out what they did for a living, and after some extensive social media stalking, search for them on LinkedIn. And then, if you started dating that person, you would repeat this procedure to uncover information on all their exes, friends and family members. You would never tell them any of this, of course. And that's just falling in love. While falling out of love might have once been as simple as saying goodbye to someone, now it requires a complete overhaul of your social media. Block, delete and unfollow, or remain forever haunted by the digital ghost of your ex-lover. The way we date now is completely different to how people dated even as little as ten years ago. And that's the case for everyone, even if they're not on social media or don't own a smartphone, because the changes that have affected dating transcend technology.

There have been some major societal shifts, such as the #MeToo movement and Brexit, that have brought about seismic changes to the way we think about relationships. Does it matter if your partner doesn't share the same political values as you? What does consent actually mean? And what qualifies as a non-consensual experience? Then the coronavirus pandemic struck and transported us to another dating era entirely. Suddenly, physical intimacy was off the table, forcing single people to slow things down and adopt archaic dating rituals such as courting. Meanwhile, non-cohabiting couples had to either go months without seeing each other or adapt to a new life where they saw each other 24/7.

Now is as good a time as any to say that *Millennial Love* is not a book that describes things that happen to all millennials. The title of this book (just as with the podcast) refers to the fact that it explores concerns that have developed alongside the millennial generation and might, in retrospect, come to be associated with them.

These pages are filled with stories. Some belong to the public figures who have been guests on my podcast, others belong to close friends, and a few belong to strangers who contacted me privately on social media. Some of the stories are also my own. For the sake of anonymity, the men included in them have been given pseudonyms, sometimes multiple ones. I have written about them with caution, aware that their experiences may differ from my own – and should any of them go on to write a book about relationships, I look forward to reading their side of the story. But this book is not for them. It is for you, dear reader. It is for anyone who has ever felt silenced in a relationship, anyone who has ever felt ridiculous for checking to see when the person they fancy was 'last active' on WhatsApp, and for anyone who has ever been ghosted, breadcrumbed, orbited, or fallen victim to any of those other ridiculous terms. This book is for anyone who has ever been told by a partner that they are 'crazy', or made to feel like they really might be, or that their experiences aren't worth sharing. Dating has officially become absurd, we should at least be able to talk about it. In the words of the American novelist Anne Lamott: 'You own everything that happened to you. Tell your stories. If people wanted you to write warmly about them, they should have behaved better.'

Chapter One
Cool Girls and Fuck Boys

I should have loved a thunderbird instead;
At least when spring comes they roar back again.
I shut my eyes and all the world drops dead.
(I think I made you up inside my head.)

Extract from *Mad Girl's Love Song*
by Sylvia Plath

If I were a Cool Girl, my love life would have been very different.
I would not have spent eight years pining after someone who
wasn't interested in me. I would not have lingered by countless
bars, waiting for someone to look at me. And I certainly would
have had sex more than twice by the time I was 23.

The Cool Girl has existed in one form or another for years,
but it was author Gillian Flynn who brought it to life most
memorably in her bestselling thriller, *Gone Girl*. Protagonist
Amy Dunne spends the first half of Flynn's novel pretending
to be someone she is not. Then, in a series of sentences, Amy
carefully dismantles the identity she's been feigning. Here's
how she describes the Cool Girl:

Men always say that as the defining compliment, don't they?
She's a cool girl. Being the Cool Girl means I am a hot, bril-

liant, funny woman who adores football, poker, dirty jokes, and burping, who plays video games, drinks cheap beer, loves threesomes and anal sex, and jams hot dogs and hamburgers into her mouth like she's hosting the world's biggest culinary gang bang while somehow maintaining a size two, because Cool Girls are above all hot. Hot and understanding. Cool Girls never get angry; they only smile in a chagrined, loving manner and let their men do whatever they want. Go ahead, shit on me, I don't mind, I'm the Cool Girl.

Women have spent a lifetime being pigeonholed into stereotypes like this. There's an entire cast of caricatures. Some are generic (Manic Pixie Dream Girls, Spinsters, Career-obsessed Bitches) and others are specific to minorities: Asian Nerds, Quirky Lesbians, Angry Black Women. The journalist and author Pandora Sykes lists these tropes and more in her book, *How Do We Know We're Doing It Right*, and explains how the flattening of the female identity in this way is 'a key element of consumer capitalism'. Once you identify a trope, you can sell something to it, she writes, which explains why we see these tropes projected in so many advertising campaigns.

But we also see these tropes operate within the dating world. At least we do in almost all the romantic comedies and TV shows I grew up watching. These two-dimensional characters were typically straight white women like me, whose existence was almost entirely shaped by the male gaze. The Manic Pixie Dream Girls (ditzy, ethereal, beguiling) were found in *Garden State*, *500 Days of Summer* and *There's Something About Mary*. The Career-obsessed Bitches (harsh, cold and married to their job) were in *The Devil Wears Prada*, *The Proposal* and *Morning Glory*. And the rest were in *Sex and the City*.

But let's go back to Cool Girls; it's a label that stands out from the rest because rather than being one that women fear, it's one they aspire towards. The Cool Girl trope was established long before Flynn's book came out and, unfortunately, is still relevant today.

How to be the perfect Cool Girl now

Don't be like other girls. Have three female friends who are not as hot as you. Wear suits. Chain smoke Marlboro Lights while maintaining perfect skin. Be French. Be the last person to leave the dinner party but the first to offer everyone high-quality cocaine. Always order fries. Be vegan. Wear matching underwear on weekdays. Do Pilates. Have no social media except for Instagram; post photos of yourself posing with your less-hot friends in an empty bath for no apparent reason. Have angular arms.

The Cool Girl is artfully examined in Elizabeth Sankey's critically acclaimed documentary, *Romantic Comedy*, in which she and a chorus of critics, actors and filmmakers discuss how some of the most popular films on love warped their perceptions of dating, romance, sex and sexuality. The documentary homes in on films like *How to Lose a Guy in 10 Days*, in which the protagonist, Andie Anderson (Kate Hudson), rejects her natural Cool Girl persona and adopts its antithesis by becoming needy and overly emotional, all so that she can repel Benjamin Barry (Matthew McConaughey) for a magazine article (spoiler: it works). Sankey's documentary also looks at how some films have experimented with the Cool Girl trope by turning it on its head; such as *Ruby Sparks*, in which a male novelist's dream woman – a stock model Cool Girl – magically comes to life after he writes about her. Once she's made real, he's able to completely control her personality, the way she dresses and the way she speaks. This, writer and star Zoe Kazan suggests, is in essence what male filmmakers have been doing for years. By having Cool Girl characters as the objects of desire in their films, the implication is that this is how a woman needs to behave in order to be considered attractive by men.

'The Cool Girl trope has been around forever,' Sankey told me. 'It just changes slightly with each generation. Women are taught from an early age to be quiet, submissive, not to make a fuss. To be diplomatic, to let things go, to not get angry. When it comes to relationships, that translates into this idea of being "easy-going". I've heard so many men complain about an ex-girlfriend who was "crazy" when I was younger and I thought, "well I'm going to do my best to make sure no ex ever describes me that way", whereas now I think, "was she crazy, or was she just expressing herself and you didn't like it?"'

Films like *How to Lose a Guy in 10 Days* amplify this toxic breed of conditioning. 'That film taught me that in order to find a man and keep him happy, a woman should be laid-back and fun,' said Sankey. 'I should never complain if my date changed plans last minute or was insensitive, I should be into the same things he's into, I should hide any insecurities I might have about myself, and I should be thin with a huge appetite. The nightmare of it is that it encourages women to pit themselves against each other. "I'm not like your crazy ex, she sounds awful, I'm so chilled and easy-going, you can treat me like shit and I won't mind." I would say that I wasn't really myself in relationships until I met my husband and finally allowed myself to drop the idea that there was a specific way I needed to be in order for him to love me.'

The Cool Girl trope is more likely to impact straight women than those of other sexualities, because it's a character designed to please men. This is one of the reasons why author and illustrator Florence Given said that she finds it so much more liberating being on a date with a woman or a non-binary person as opposed to being on a date with a man because she doesn't have to 'perform a gender role'. 'There's so much freedom to just show up and be my authentic self,' Given said when she came on the podcast. 'As opposed to when I'm on a date with a man, which I don't do very often, it's entirely different because you're constantly, or subconsciously anyway, performing around his masculinity. At least, that's what I felt and realised I was doing after I journaled about it. I felt like I was going into a shrinking machine designed to cater to his ego, and the version of myself that he would love the most.'

When author and journalist Dolly Alderton came on the podcast, she confessed to being very good at 'doing the Cool Girl act', particularly in the early stages of dating someone. 'Men never knew how much of a psychopath I was,' she teased. Like so many women I know, including myself, she had mastered the art of feigning disinterest in men who she was consumed by. It's something many of us do: send one text when we want to send twenty, say we're busy on nights when we're not, and act surprised when they talk about the holiday we already know all about from Instagram.

I have never been terribly good at playing the part of the Cool Girl. I once dated a guy called Zack. We met on Bumble and had two fantastic dates together – one was at a cosy Soho pub, famous for being poet Dylan Thomas's haunt, and the other was at an Italian speakeasy, both of which were pretentious enough to impress me. But Zack and I didn't work out. Maybe it was because he was in the middle of exams, or because he purported to be too old fashioned to subscribe to modern methods of communication – he took regular breaks from social media. Whatever the reason, his distance obviously only made me fancy him more. So, I got creative. Here's a selection of messages I sent Zack when I felt him pulling away: 'Lord Byron would have had his incel moments', 'I know about a lot of naughty things' and 'The world would be a better place if all worm dance moves were heartfelt and carefully orchestrated'. And, because I wasn't going to go out without a fight, here's a selection of texts I sent Zack when he stopped replying to me: 'You're not so into this phone business are you?', 'I've pretty much forgotten what you look like at this point' and 'Apologies for getting in touch on WhatsApp, I know you would've preferred a more rustic method, but owl mail is unavailable past 8pm'.

Being the Cool Girl is not just about playing it cool. You can lose yourself in the persona you create, which will vary depending on the man you're trying to be a Cool Girl for. If he supports Chelsea FC, the Cool Girl will post Frank Lampard memes on Twitter. If he's into French New Wave, the Cool Girl will get a fringe. If he likes eighteenth-century literature, the Cool Girl will have books about the Age of Enlightenment in her bedroom. I tried very hard to adopt a lot of these roles. So much so, in fact, that for a long time, I couldn't work out which parts of myself I had crafted for a man, and which were my own. I recently looked back at some of my old Spotify playlists and found so many that had been curated to suit the tastes of the man I was dating at the time. I don't listen to any of those songs now.

Take the time I dated a guy called Mark who really wanted people to know that he was left wing; he had a Momentum sticker on his laptop and his Hinge profile proudly stated that he had 'never kissed a Tory'. Mark also lived in a two-bedroom flat in central London that his dad bought for him, by the way. I knew embarrassingly little about politics at the time, but I really fancied Mark – even if he was a raging champagne socialist – and I needed him to fancy me. So, I ordered a copy of *British Politics for Dummies* from Amazon and got to work. Mark's Cool Girl needed to be a connoisseur in everything from Churchill to the Iraq War – even if she hadn't opened a history book since the age of 13.

If you pretend to be a Cool Girl for too long, you will get caught out. It was all going well with Mark until he started talking about the then-Labour MP Chuka Umunna. Only Mark didn't say he was a Labour MP. For all I knew, Chuka Umunna could have been an up-and-coming saxophonist with a passion for liberal politics. Far too embarrassed to ask who he was when Mark started talking about him, I nodded and pretended to know exactly who Chuka Umunna was. It worked until Mark asked what I thought of Chuka's latest column in a national newspaper. 'Oh, it was great. I agreed with every point. What do you fancy for dinner?' Then he asked if I agreed with the bits about the EU. 'Of course. I'm thinking pizza?' Then he asked about the part on Keynesian economics. 'I don't know much about Kenya. Franco Manca?' Mark dumped me two weeks later, and I gave my copy of *British Politics for Dummies* to a charity shop.

If you've ever felt like you want to be a Cool Girl as Flynn describes it – let's call her the stock Cool Girl – chances are it's because you think you've actually met someone like this. The woman who really does love anal sex (never done it, never will) as much as pizza and swallows her partner's come (the one time I did this, I vomited) before washing it down with cheap beer. At my university, I branded countless women as Cool Girls. They would line the bar in my student halls, beer in one hand, packet of liquorice Rizla filters in the other. While I was standing awkwardly by the ping pong table sipping vodka lime sodas – I'd heard they were the most slimming drink – having insipid conversations about gap years, the Cool Girls were slunk reclining in corners, Coronas in hand, trading tales about older men who fancied them. Most of these women knew each other before university and were in tight-knit cliques, bonded by their wealthy upbringings, second-hand designer wardrobes and the fact they all had names like Foxy and Fluff. They had cohorts of male friends, too, all of whom wanted to sleep with them. I tried to befriend one called Bing (I never found out her real name). She was sitting next to me in an English seminar and I asked where her jacket was from. 'It's vintage Dior but I found it in a budget bin in a charity shop in Rio.' I tried to ask why she was in Rio but by the time I had wrapped my head around someone throwing a Dior jacket into a budget bin, she had turned to talk to her friend about a guy called Otis who was rubbish at fingering. Perhaps Bing was just pretentious, rude, blind to her privilege, or all three. But all the boys at my university fancied her and not me. She was still Cool. And I hated her for it. That's the trouble with Cool Girls: if you believe they exist, you will loathe them because you are not them. Like Sankey said, the concept pits women against one another by perpetuating a hierarchy of attractiveness that places Cool Girls at the top and everyone else at the bottom. This meant that I couldn't bear the Cool Girls – until one became my best friend.

Lydia wasn't in the Bing crew; she was more of a loner, but still cool to her core. She made her own clothes, danced like Shakira and had long blonde hair that was in dire need of a wash but still somehow looked glamorous. Men gravitated towards Lydia like bees to a sunflower. We couldn't have been more different. I liked organisation; Lydia craved chaos. I was the first one to leave a party; Lydia was the last. I questioned everything I said before I said it; Lydia simply spoke. On our second night at university, a boy called Max was trying to work out which celebrity she looked like. I fancied Max. But after a few minutes of the three of us talking, I got the sense he would rather I left so he could carry on flirting with my friend. I was tenacious (and drunk), so I stayed. 'I've got it!' Max cried, finally working out who it was that Lydia looked like. 'Gisele!' he said as Lydia erupted into a fit of giggles – as if the idea of her looking like a supermodel was that far-fetched. 'Who am I?' I asked. Max looked at me for the first time in the entire conversation. 'You look like the woman who sells engagement rings on QVC. She has nice hands.' I do quite like my hands – and I'm sure the woman on QVC is lovely – so this didn't bother me too much, but I suspect it would have felt better to have been compared to a supermodel.

I couldn't understand why Lydia wanted to be friends with me, but we bonded quickly over a mutual hatred of organised fun – I still don't get Pub Golf – and a mutual love of flared trousers and velvet. Our conversations quickly turned to love, and I realised that even though Lydia had been in relationships before (I hadn't) and was far more sexually experienced than me (I was still a virgin at 18), we had many of the same anxieties and neuroses about dating. She had just broken up with someone and was unsure whether it was the right time to move on with the guy down the hall who already fancied her (note that we'd only been at uni for four days). I had a crush on a boy in the block opposite ours but was pretty sure he was sleeping with the warden. This was the dynamic – her pondering whom to reject, me pondering whom to pine after – but it worked.

Being friends with Lydia taught me that Cool Girls don't exist beyond the periphery. But this is the problem: the periphery is the space in which we now date. It was easy for me to fake it with Mark because I'd only known him for four weeks. And, like Zack, I had met him on a dating app, where you can be whoever you want; whether it's a Cool Girl who designs their own clothes, one who makes terrible jokes about owl mail, or one who reads everything Chuka Umunna writes. Your identity is yours to optimise via the photos you select for your profile, the information you choose to share in your bio and those first few messages you spend hours agonising over. The same goes for Instagram, one of the first places people go to get more information about someone they've just met. Scroll through someone's Insta and you'll get a carousel of filtered photographs and fastidiously considered captions, chosen by someone who wants you to think that this is who they are. But that carousel will never paint an authentic picture of that person because Instagram, the same as dating app profiles, is about personal branding. It's about creating a version of yourself that people will like. And, given the option, why would you be your insecurity-ridden self, when you could just as easily be a glossy, sparkly Cool Girl?

When we discussed Cool Girls on the podcast, a lot of listeners asked what the equivalent was for men. And the truth is that there isn't one. Because the Cool Girl is an idea fuelled by societal ills that men don't experience to the same degree as women, namely sexism. But it's also about the way women are conditioned: to be people-pleasers. The poet Charly Cox, raised this on the podcast when we discussed why women tolerate being treated poorly in relationships. 'We're constantly told that we have to be liked,' she said. 'You've got to be the soft girl, the funny girl, the pretty girl. Then the problem is that you find someone that likes you enough and you're like, "Okay, how do I keep up this facade?"'

So, there are no Cool Guys, so to speak. But there are Fuck Boys – lots of them. The term 'Fuck Boy' originates from hip-hop culture; rapper Cam'ron was the first artist to use it in passing in his 2002 track 'Boy, Boy'. But it didn't make its way to the mainstream until 2014, when Google searches of the phrase spiked. This was around the same time that American hip-hop duo Run the Jewels released their track 'Oh My Darling Don't Cry', which featured lyrics such as: 'That fuckboy life about to be repealed. That fuckboy shit about to be repelled.' Since then, the phrase has featured in countless songs about womanisers and has subsequently become common parlance among millennials to refer to a man who sleeps with women he has no intention of pursuing a relationship with, despite his behaviour indicating otherwise. But the term has acquired countless other meanings, too, and is often used to describe a set of behaviours far more damaging than simply enjoying casual sex.

How to be the perfect Fuck Boy now

Tell people you are really bad on your phone and you need to sort your life out (never actually sort your life out or stop being really bad on your phone). Poke people on Facebook but don't message them. Pontificate about the futility of 'labelling' a relationship. Reply 'hellooooo' whenever someone tries to make plans with you. Don't talk about your family or ask about anyone else's. Use the phrase 'we were hanging out' to describe every relationship you've ever had. Spend two weeks telling someone they are the most amazing person you've ever met, then block them and move to Mexico. Have messy hair, or no hair at all.

Every straight woman I know has dated a Fuck Boy. These are the men who treat women like toys. They are terrible at communication, have commitment issues and typically have an expiration date of two months before they're off being someone else's Fuck Boy. But, because nothing in the dating world can ever be simple, Fuck Boys can also be kind, complimentary and, well, really, *really* hot. Hence why we're so quick to defend them. YouTuber Lucy Moon addressed this dilemma when we spoke about a Fuck Boy she had dated. 'He lied to me constantly,' she said. 'And I was just so sick of it to the point where I was like, "Well I don't want to sleep with you at all anymore." Then he did a full routine of guilt-tripping and emotional blackmail to convince me I had made it all up and he really liked me. That was confusing.' It's the second part of Moon's story that made her partner a Fuck Boy. Here was not a man who just treated a woman badly. Here was a man who treated a woman badly and then manipulated her so she would think he had done nothing wrong. He made it so that Moon would be the one questioning her behaviour, not him. Had she overreacted? Could she have been a bit melodramatic? Or maybe even unfair? That's the thing about Fuck Boys: they pretend to be the good guys.

Fuck Boys are flourishing in the modern dating scene, where new technologies have created countless opportunities for them to behave poorly. But the way that Fuck Boys behave is subtle; they won't recognise their behaviour as cruel and will brush off claims that it is with phrases like 'you're overreacting'. Many of the Fuck Boys' favoured tactics have names – e.g. 'haunting' (when someone likes your social media posts long after you've stopped dating them) and 'R-bombing' (reading your message and not replying, whilst knowing you can see it's been read thanks to read receipts). These are both classic Fuck Boy behaviours. For the sake of ease – and fun – let's call them Fuckboyeries. One of the most brutal Fuckboyeries is 'breadcrumbing', which Collins Dictionary defines as 'dropping hints to someone that you are interested in them romantically with no intention of following through'. This happened to me when I dated a Fuck Boy called Justin. He had all the classic signs of a Fuck Boy from the start: keen, polite, nice hair and terrible at communication. We had been dating for around two months when he told me he was going to Canada for five weeks and the signal would be patchy, but he'd love to see me when he got back. We kissed goodbye outside Kentish Town tube station, and I went home feeling confident that, in five weeks' time, I would have a boyfriend called Justin. I didn't hear from him for six months. But even though Justin hadn't messaged me, he liked all my Instagram posts, including ones of me in a bikini. Every like (or breadcrumb) from Justin made me think it was only a matter of time until he got in touch asking to meet for a drink so we could dive back headfirst into our dizzying romance. In fact, when he did eventually get in touch, it was to ask if I had any contacts for getting tickets to Glastonbury.

The Fuck Boy has become an integral part of our dating jargon, but it's also one that needs to be examined, possibly now more than ever. When you give something a name, it becomes normalised. The problem is that the Fuck Boy is a gendered – and typically heteronormative – term, so this behaviour is only really normalised for straight men, despite the very obvious fact that people of any gender or sexuality can be just as cruel and manipulative. I've treated men badly before. I'm pretty sure I've even dropped a few R-bombs in my time, and I know I'm not the only one. So why is it Fuck Boy and not Fuck Girl? Or better yet, the much more politically correct Fuck Person. To answer this, let's take a look at popular culture.

In *Cruel Intentions*, it was Sebastian Valmont, a character who wooed women with lines like, 'God you're beautiful, I'm going to take you to lunch' and who would later decry these same women 'insipid Manhattan debutantes'. In *Bridget Jones's Diary*, it was Daniel Cleaver. And in *Alfie*, it was, well, Alfie. These characters cheat, lie, schmooze and manipulate their way into women's lives. And yet their actions almost always seem vindicated – if not glorified – thanks to charisma, charm, or really good hair. TV shows are littered with Fuck Boys too – he's Chuck Bass in *Gossip Girl*, Damon Salvatore in *The Vampire Diaries*, Christian Troy in *Nip/Tuck* – and so is music, where songs like Robin Thicke's 'Blurred Lines' erode female autonomy and present sex as something that men do to women with or without their consent. The issue is that, despite this,

'Blurred Lines' was a number one track, just as every TV show and film I've mentioned here has been a huge hit. These attitudes and characters are so ingrained in us socially and culturally that we often don't even question them. Hence why some women expect men to behave like Fuck Boys, and men sometimes expect it from themselves.

Jordan Stephens, actor and Rizzle Kicks singer, told me that he used to be a Fuck Boy. 'I needed to face some really hard truths about my own behaviour,' he said, explaining how #MeToo forced him to reconsider how he had acted in previous relationships. 'I have never physically assaulted anyone. But I had deep intimacy and commitment issues and I can also recognise my own emotional neglect and coercive control.' I asked Stephens what he thought about the fact that these behavioural patterns are more attached to men than to women. 'It's very damaging to men and we don't want anything to do with them, but it's a space created by societal expectations,' he replied, before going on to discuss what he thought was the root cause of these societal expectations. 'The male sex is more physically dominant, just biologically. And in my mind, that leads to a sense of entitlement and an abuse of power.' If you truly believe that men and women are equal, as I do, Stephens's theory might be hard to swallow, because it requires you to acknowledge the physical superiority that men have over women and accept that this superiority breeds hubris – the kind of hubris that entitles a man to treat a woman like crap (I'll touch on abuse in Chapter Eight), or, in other words, to be a Fuck Boy. At least, that was Stephens's argument.

If you've ever been with a Fuck Boy, you will know that getting rid of them is easier said than done. These are the men our friends tell us to dump, ignore and move on from.

Simple. Except it never is, because after a certain point, the manipulation, game-playing and perpetual ricochet between hot and cold starts to have an impact, and before you know it, the Fuck Boy is the boy you want the most *because* you can't have him. When this is something you've been feeling for longer than just a few months, it begs some harsh questions. Why are you keeping this person around? How much of the pain you've suffered at their hands have you facilitated? Or romanticised, or even created? These are all questions I've been asking myself for years.

Jack didn't seem like a Fuck Boy at first. He was in the year above me at school. He had honey-coloured curls and a dry sense of humour. I was 14 when we were introduced by my friend Lucy; she and Jack had been messaging on MSN and she'd asked me to tag along to meet him and another guy from school one afternoon. Lucy decided she preferred the look of the other guy and told me I could 'have' Jack if I wanted. I didn't, but we became friends and soon found out we lived in the same pocket of north London. We started going for walks in the evenings after school, poking fun at each other's habits and sharing stories about our divorced parents. Soon we were meeting most nights and texting furiously in between. We didn't kiss, I'm not really sure why. Nonetheless, our conversations were intimate enough that it felt like we were dating. Or, at least, it did until one night I kissed one of his friends at a party. It was a drunken mistake, one I deeply regretted. But it was enough for Jack to call it quits on our almost-relationship. I was devastated. When we arrived back at school the following September, I was sure he'd want to give things a go between us, for real this time. But the only thing Jack wanted to do was spend time with his new girlfriend, who, unfortunately for me but fortunately for her, had legs like Kate Moss and a face from a L'Oréal campaign.

I was in my final year of school when Jack messaged me on Facebook to ask if I'd like to go for a 'spin' in his new car around our local area. It had been two years since we'd spoken, and despite what I'd told myself and my friends, my feelings for him had never wavered. So, I went for the spin. After that, we met every few weeks. He'd ask me out for coffee and complain about his girlfriend, who had become 'difficult'. I'd pretend to like the coffee and listen to him moan about how his Kate Moss-alike didn't clean up after herself and was a bit rude to his mum. I convinced myself that I was more of a catch than her. I'm clean, friendly to mums and an all-round better person. I was the one he should be with, not her.

On the surface, our meetings were harmless. We never got too close and barely even hugged to say hello or goodbye. But I would always leave recounting the details – every conversation, every question, every glance – as if they meant something. Something massive that I could never quite articulate. One night, Jack asked to meet for a drink at the pub. It was the first time one of our meetings involved alcohol. It felt weird. He sat next to me on a tiny bench outside, offered me his scarf when I was cold, and at my door after walking me home, he kissed me. The next day, a text: 'I've been waiting for that kiss for six years. I can't deny that I have feelings for you.'

I didn't hear from him for months after that. Facebook messages and texts went unanswered; phone calls rang to voicemail. It wasn't until a mutual friend's party six months later that I saw him again. But he didn't even acknowledge me until we left and got on the same bus to go home. Strangely, the minute we were away from the group, we were back in our groove and catching up as if nothing had happened. At my door, we kissed again.

The next few years followed a similar pattern of events. Jack and I would go months without speaking, but every now and then, his name would light up my phone with a joke about our local pub, or about a tweet I'd posted. Sometimes he'd congratulate me on work achievements, or even wish me a happy birthday. I analysed the minutiae of every message he ever sent, from the wording to the grammar. Occasionally, we would go for drinks and catch up but nothing ever happened between us. We bumped into each other a few times, too, and I'd find something to hold onto every time. Like the moment from a 21st birthday party, when he said that if we had stayed together as teenagers, we'd probably still have been together then. Or the time we spotted each other at the pub, when he shared a secret he claimed to have never told anyone else. My friends told me I was nuts for holding onto a silly teenage crush and that Jack was only ever being friendly and polite. Maybe he was, but I found transcendent meaning in everything he ever said to me. We never spoke about who we were dating, though I eventually heard he and Kate Moss-alike had broken up, which fit neatly into the narrative I was forming in my head. Jack and I were meant to be together, but we would have to overcome a few hurdles first because that's just how love works – it's supposed to take time. It's supposed to be complicated – and it means more if it is.

Jack and I don't really talk anymore. Occasionally, I'll check in with him to see how he's doing, and he'll reply in his polite way. But he won't ever initiate a conversation with me. Over time, he stopped asking to meet me for drinks, and whenever

I asked him, he would say yes and then cancel at the last minute. The 'happy birthday' texts eventually dried up too, as did the sporadic jokes. I still don't know how to describe what happened between us. To me, Jack was a significant person in my life for a very long time. He was someone I cared about, respected and really liked. But was it love, or infatuation? And was he a Fuck Boy? Or did I turn him into one to rationalise my obsession with our nonexistent relationship? Even now, I can't answer any of these questions, because I never knew how Jack felt about me, or if any of the things that meant so much to me meant anything to him. I still don't.

Chapter Two
Getting your Kicks
from Blue Ticks

When David said he was 'going phoneless for a few days', I pretended to be jealous. 'Oh cool, I'd love to go phoneless,' I replied glibly. 'What a great idea. Enjoy the solitude.' In reality, I was hurt and a bit dumbstruck. David and I might have only been on four dates, but I was already thinking about whether he'd prefer a fish or vegetarian starter at our wedding. I arrogantly assumed he felt the same, but the fact that he didn't want to talk to anyone, including me, for a few days implied otherwise. I decided this must be David's way of calling it quits and I should appreciate that he was at least kind enough to make up an elaborate lie about why he would no longer be texting me.

The average person spends three hours and fifteen minutes on their phone every day, which actually doesn't sound like very much. But think about it. If you aren't using your phone, chances are it's in your pocket, on your desk at work while you use a computer, or on the dinner table while you eat. We are rarely far away from screens for longer than a few minutes. In this hyper-connected world, society expects us to be contactable at all times because we usually are – which is why the default status on WhatsApp is literally 'available'. We operate within an ouroboros of communication, so when someone withdraws from that, like David, it can seem odd, namely because, short of getting into a time machine and going back to the nineteenth century, *it's not possible*.

Before David's digital departure, he'd asked me to send over a few of my articles for him to read when he returned. I immediately drafted a message in my iPhone Notes presenting him with three articles that I'd carefully selected based on his interests. I waited four days to send it, thinking he would no longer be phoneless by then. But my WhatsApp message did not deliver, prompting just one sad lonely looking grey tick where there should have been two bright blue ones. David had probably hidden his phone in a cupboard under the stairs. Maybe he had even lost it, or it had been stolen. This was to be expected. This was okay. This was FINE.

Two days passed, and that single grey tick was still staring me in the face. That's when I Googled: 'How do you know if you've been blocked on WhatsApp?'. Google told me that if I'd been blocked, I would see a single grey tick next to my message.

The thought that someone could find me so repulsive that they couldn't even bear to receive my messages made me physically unwell with insecurities. Of course, I'd heard of this happening. You go on a few dates with someone, you think it's going really well and then out of nowhere, they end all communication. You feel sad, pathetic and humiliated and your friends will tell their friends that they 'knew a girl who got ghosted'. After a week, that grey tick was haunting me to the point where I could think of little else. Everything suddenly seemed grey, from the outside of the tube to the takeaway coffee cup in my office canteen. I swear to god I even found a grey pube. WHY WAS EVERYTHING GREY? While I was busy seeing grey all around, David had probably met someone else. Someone who wasn't spending their evenings asking Google questions like: 'Why do people ghost you?', 'What does ghosting say about you?' and 'How do you know if you're dating a sociopath?'.

I told myself I just wasn't ready for a relationship and that David clearly wasn't ready either. And that this was all for the best because I was a strong independent woman who did not need a man. Especially not one like David. Two weeks later, I was running out of platitudes. That's when I saw it. That single grey tick had become a double grey tick. Two hours later, those two ticks turned blue. David had finally read my message. I yelped out loud. 'GUYS,' I texted the 'Cock Warriors' WhatsApp group I'm in with four of my closest friends, Lola, Ella, Bethan and Lexi – one of Ella's ex-boyfriends chose the name of the group six years ago and for some reason we've never changed it. 'He read my message. I am not a hideously unfunny and unattractive baboon.' They congratulated me and we all revelled in my newfound feelings of joy and self-assurance. David did not reply for another five days.

For all intents and purposes, there is nothing wrong with read receipts. They are a perfunctory part of our digitised lives: it is useful to know when a colleague has not yet read an urgent work memo, it is helpful to see when a relative has not yet received your invitation to lunch. But it is absolutely agonising to know when someone you fancy has not yet read your pun about cheese. Or worse, that they have read it and ignored it for five days. Despite seeming innocuous, read receipts can contribute hugely to the amount of anxiety we experience in relationships. They first appeared on Apple products in 2011, but now are on almost every mainstream social media platform, including WhatsApp, Instagram and Facebook, which owns the aforementioned two. Many people have written about how read receipts hinder our mental wellbeing generally, but few have explored how the consequences are multiplied tenfold when we apply this to relationships.

In the early stages of dating someone – a state often referred to as infatuation – we are already anxious. We question every conversation and comment, giving our insecurities ample space to blossom. And because flirtation rewards ambiguity – everything is hotter when it is implied rather than clarified – we often have no idea whether another person's feelings are developing in the same way as ours. We tangle ourselves into a web of self-doubt, asking questions like: 'Did I sound pretentious when I was talking about my favourite books?', 'Did I ask too many questions about their family?' and 'Did I talk too much about *my* family?'. Throw instant messaging into the mix, and that cacophony of questions is amplified to a deafening degree because it gives us so many more questions to ask.

The main issue with read receipts is that they have made it possible for us to see when we are being ignored. It is the equivalent of going up to someone, asking them a question, and then watching them walk away from you with no explanation at all. Sure, that person might have a meeting to attend, a phone call to take, or a marble cake to take out of the oven. But you don't know that without being told. All you can see is the cold hard proof that your message did not warrant an immediate response. And that can feel crippling when you are attracted to that person, because all you want to do is talk to them, learn about them and share things with them. It would be nice to know that they feel the same way about you but leaving your message on 'read' implies that they have something better to do. And so it makes you want their attention more.

The model Immy Waterhouse described this feeling to me as a 'microtrauma'. 'Even with or without the "read" receipt, after a certain amount of time you know they've seen it because we are all glued to our phones. When someone leaves my message on "read", I stew and start to convince myself they must've got in an accident or died. And as the hours roll on and turn into days, you swallow the hard pill of truth that it just maybe wasn't meant to be.'

These insecurities and frustrations aren't exclusive to single people, either. Author and journalist Lisa Taddeo told me she gets annoyed when her husband of eight years reads and doesn't respond to her texts. 'He's seen it, it's a question that's important to me, and whether or not he knows the answer, or wants to deal with me – for example, "Have you taught our daughter the math lesson for today?" – and he has not, he doesn't want to reply until, perhaps, he's done it, to avoid my wrath. But that hurts my feelings. I want him to reply, "No I haven't yet, but I will soon." Or even: "No, and I don't feel like it." Because the latter two replies acknowledge me, my question. But that's not quite the thing you're asking.'

Things get particularly complicated when you bring multiple messaging platforms into the mix. Comedian and podcaster James Barr used to spend hours agonising over the fact that his boyfriend would leave him unread on WhatsApp all day, so he'd look to see when he was last active on Instagram. 'He was almost always "last active" two minutes ago,' he told me.

'I was like, "I'm being ghosted by my own boyfriend." Obviously, it's not exactly "healthy" to be obsessively checking up on anyone's Instagram activity all day, which is why I'd also look at when he was last active on Facebook Messenger and Snapchat. At times I even re-downloaded happn (the dating app we met on) to check if he'd been back online to search for someone new.' Barr put his anxiety down to a fear of being cheated on. 'It's a constant fear and I will think about the same thing over and over again until I've found substantial evidence to prove myself right. Ultimately, the fact that my then-boyfriend never found the time to reply to a hot picture of me in a jock strap would send me into such a bitch fit that I decided to break my anxiety loop by calling him. "How have you found time to double tap a man with a yucca between his legs on @boyswithplants, and NOT send a text to your own boyfriend?!" Silence. Of course, there's no logical answer to this question. Maybe he just likes plants? Or maybe he's not that into me. Either way, he and I broke up. I realised, irrational or not, I needed a reply – and that I respect myself enough to know that my flower is more important.'

Of course, it works the opposite way too. Let's say you're trying to play hard-to-get. Better yet, let's say you're playing the role of a Cool Girl. What better way to feign insouciance than by ignoring someone's messages? Like I said, seeming unavailable will (most likely) only make someone like you more.

It's strange how much meaning we attach to response times. For many, they have become a measure of how interested in us someone is, like in Barr's case, or, as in Taddeo's case, how committed they are to us. If someone we like replies instantly, we interpret that as the ultimate validation that they like us too. Then if they are slow at replying, we may assume they don't feel the same way. Or worse, that they are simply indifferent, which can be just as upsetting.

For me, this way of thinking originated in my teenage years, when my friends and I played something now commonly known as 'The Waiting Game'. If you don't know what this is, or insist you've never played it, you are either wrong or simply in denial. We have all played this game. Traditionally speaking, 'The Waiting Game' dictates that you should match somebody's response time and raise it. For example, if the person you're pining after takes twenty minutes to reply, you should then take a minimum of thirty minutes. If they take five minutes, you're allowed to reply seven minutes later, but it would be best to wait a bit longer. In fact, the longer you can wait, the better. All this, the game suggests, will imply that you are breezy, busy and important. It makes you seem unavailable, intriguing and, well, hot. Of course, this is really just inane, absurd and, well, juvenile. But I like to believe that it is only natural, because I've been playing this game my whole life.

A few years ago, I met a very hot photographer at a fancy magazine party I had absolutely no business being at. We crossed paths for a few minutes by the loo and managed to maintain a flirtatious rapport on WhatsApp. It wasn't enough to facilitate a real-life meeting, but it was certainly enough for me to fantasise about the sprawling Beverly Hills mansion we'd live in after we got married in a French chateau with a walk-in fridge stocked with lots of very pale rosé. I played the game perfectly. If he took twenty-two minutes to reply to my last message, I'd take twenty-five. If he took four, I'd take six – ten if I was feeling particularly nonchalant. And so forth.

When he eventually stopped replying to me, I was gutted. So much so, that two days later, when my message asking about his weekend plans was still just blue-ticked, I committed the cardinal sin of instant messaging. I sent another message. He read it almost immediately but still did not reply. Three days later, I sent another message. And then I sent one more. I was a woman possessed.

The double, triple, and in my case, quadruple, message is something your friends will strongly advise against. It is so deeply uncool that I'm almost hoping you have skim read this chapter so that I can save some face. The humiliation I felt after the photographer failed to respond to all four of my messages was unbearable. I wanted to bring my knees close to my chest, bow my head, throw a duvet over the top and stay there until my cheeks stopped burning. I deleted our entire conversation and tried to pretend it had never happened. The worst part of the entire saga was that I know how it feels to receive a double message (I can't say I've ever received a triple, let alone a quadruple message), and the conclusions I often jump to aren't kind. Words that spring to mind include 'keen', 'creepy', and the worst word of all, 'desperate'. Nobody wants to hear those words attached to their name. So why do we double message?

I put this question to my Cock Warriors group and a few other friends. 'I double message because I'm an impatient fucker,' replied one person. 'Also, I'd rather know for sure if I'm being avoided or not.' Another friend told me that she would never double message because she would hate for someone to know that she was definitely interested in them. 'It completely ruins the mystique,' she said. 'It's not sexy when you know someone is definitely into you.' All the men I spoke to insisted they would never send a double message, bar one. 'I don't care about coming across as needy because I know I'm not,' he said. 'If I send another message, it's because I have something else to say and I want to say it.'

But what about receiving a double message? 'If it's from someone I'm just talking to on a dating app, I think it's a bit weird,' said one person. 'We're not logged into dating apps as often as we are with WhatsApp or Instagram. I don't even have my notifications turned on for Hinge. But if the double message comes from someone I've been on a date with, or met before, it would be fine. It's just not very attractive, because I would interpret that to mean that they definitely like me, and that could put me off.'

Out of everyone I spoke to, the consensus was that sending a double message is not game over, but it's also not great. Context, however, is important. When you are mid-flow with somebody – let's say you've been having a flirty back-and-forth about aubergine emojis – and then they suddenly stop replying, it jars. So perhaps you send a follow-up message because you want to give them another opportunity to reply by starting a different line of conversation. Another, very valid, reason for sending a double message is to correct a typo. Or to clarify a thought. But sometimes, as Immy Waterhouse said, you just want to send another message to check that the person you've been texting has not died. In case you were wondering, the photographer did not reply to any of my messages. And he had not died – I Googled it. I mourned the loss of our bougie French wedding over a bottle of very pale rosé.

There's no escaping the pitfalls of modern communication. Even if someone like David does 'go phoneless' for a few days (I'm still not sure how anyone can do this without losing their friends and their job), they will soon have to return to being 'phonefull'. And as for those who think they can escape the wily clutches of instant messaging by turning off their read receipts, think again. There is another equally frustrating feature that allows you to see when users were 'last active' on a platform (WhatsApp, Facebook and Instagram all have this feature), which essentially tells you exactly what a read receipt does: that someone has seen your message but decided to reply to someone else's text instead of yours. You can turn this feature off, too, thankfully. But the psychological warfare doesn't end there. No matter how many features you switch off on any instant messaging platform, you can almost always see when someone is 'online' or 'live' on it, which, in some ways, is the most *Black Mirror*-esque feature of all.

Imagine you're messaging someone on WhatsApp. You're taking your time and maybe thinking of ways to ask them out. You get as far as: 'Could be fun to meet soon. You free on . . .' when suddenly the word 'online' pops up next to their profile picture. OH MY GOD THEY CAN SEE ME. CAN THEY SEE ME? CAN THEY SEE WHAT I'VE WRITTEN? CAN THEY SEE INTO MY BRAIN? When faced with such scenarios, I have been known to drop my phone in some unfortunate places, including the toilet and the bath – and once on my face.

On a lot of mainstream messaging platforms, you can also see when someone starts (and stops) typing a message to you. I fear that we've become so used to this kind of invasive style of communicating, that we don't even question it anymore. But we desperately need to. Because being able to see the exact moment that somebody begins formulating a thought is not just completely unnecessary, it's fucking weird. With this feature (which cannot be turned off on most platforms), we are essentially inviting Bob from Bumble to waddle into our psyche, make himself a cup of tea, and rifle through our underwear drawer. To put it another way, it's a major infringement on our innermost thoughts. The way we speak is public, but the way we think is private. At least, it's supposed to be.

On iMessage, you see a speech bubble containing an ellipsis when someone is typing a message to you. Charly Cox described this to me as 'visual anxiety ramping up, three dots at a time'. 'Unless it's a friend about to come out with some insatiable gossip, I have to exit the message as soon as I've sent mine,' she said. The anxieties become worse when she sees someone stop typing and then start again, only for a message never to appear. 'What did they decide they couldn't tell me? What's so harsh that needs editing? The possibilities my brain is capable of making up are absurd and immediately puts my head into a washing machine of self-hatred. Imagine if you could see the cogs of someone's brain formulating a response in a face-to-face conversation – I don't think I'd ever say anything again.'

Instant messaging is not new. When I was 10, my friends and I would come home from school and assemble on MSN messenger, where we'd remain until it started to get light outside. There, within the confines of this glorious chatroom on which people had usernames like 'lilmizmiller' and 'wonderwall4eva', we would talk freely without the prying ears or eyes of our parents. It was thrilling.

But it's impossible to compare that to the instant messaging experience today. Because, back then, instant messaging was a much more conscious activity. In order to use MSN, for example, you had to sit down in front of your computer, open the programme and keep it open for as long as you were using it. Now, given that our phones are almost always with us, we have become passive communicators. Our phones are almost always by our side. We don't need to be on WhatsApp, Facebook, Instagram or any other platform in order to receive a notification from it. We are contactable 24/7. This is why it makes no sense when someone says, 'I'm so sorry I haven't replied, I'm just really shit with my phone.' That sentence is paradoxical. By dint of having a phone, you are contactable. On MSN, you might've missed a message had you not been logged in at the time, but this is not the case for messages sent on a phone because – and here's the real *Black Mirror* bit – *you are never not logged in*.

I've heard the 'I'm shit with my phone' line so many times. Not just from Fuck Boys (see previous chapter) but from friends, too. It's only recently that I've realised it has absolutely nothing to do with being good or bad with your phone. In fact, this phrase is about arrogance. Sheer unadulterated arrogance that leads a person to believe their time is more valuable than someone else's. It's one thing to read a message and reply a few hours later when you're out of a meeting or have finished having dinner with a friend. But it is another entirely to leave a series of messages unread for several days without any explanation other than your self-diagnosed phone-shitness. What makes it even worse is that by resorting to the 'I'm shit with my phone' excuse, you absolve yourself of responsibility. And people like me fall for it every goddamn time.

The irony of all this is that instant messaging is supposed to make it easier to talk to someone. When you can send and receive messages in seconds, it more closely resembles a real-life interaction. One thought can simply unfurl onto another with effortless succession. This is how instant messaging platforms are meant to be used. And when you do use them this way in dating, without playing 'The Waiting Game' or leaving someone's messages on 'read', it can be brilliant, mostly because it is spontaneous and therefore gives your conversation a greater sense of verisimilitude. You can react to things quickly and more authentically as opposed to stewing for hours over how best to phrase something and/or sending a drafted message to various WhatsApp groups for pre-approval – I almost always do this in the early stages of dating someone.

The point is that instant messaging will not necessarily hinder your relationship, so long as you and your partner use it in similar ways. Texting compatibility is an under-explored subject when it comes to relationships, which is odd considering how vital it is to the success of one. If you are someone who prefers to reply quickly, you will expect quick replies back. Likewise, if you are someone who prefers to take your time and reply to someone hours or days later, you may struggle to empathise when someone wants you to be faster. The length of your messages matter, too. For those who communicate at a slower pace, you may prefer to send longer and more considered messages. While those in the quick-reply category might send shorter and more off-the-cuff messages.

When I spoke about this on the podcast with writer Jack May, he made the point that how someone uses their phone and engages in digital communication is indicative of who they are. 'It's strange to talk about messaging as if it's some kind of separate thing that's detached from who you are as a person. Obviously, how you message and how you communicate is going to be totally tied in with your personality. So, if you do it completely differently, it probably either suggests that you're totally different people, or that one of you likes the other person a lot less.' Ironically, if it is the latter, we will often tell ourselves it is the former because this is an easier truth to swallow. Here are some of the excuses people often come up with in this scenario: 'They are more of a phone call person', 'They'd rather speak to me in person' and 'They think instant messaging is "too mainstream"'. May said he has often told himself such things when someone has been slow to reply to him. 'What was actually happening was that the other guy wasn't that interested. And I think it's very easy to make those kinds of defences like, "oh he just uses Facebook Messenger in a different way to me and he replies to me once a day and that's fine". Then actually four weeks later, when you're still going through the Ben and Jerry's by yourself, that's when you wake up.'

At the time of recording that episode, I was dating someone who didn't have a smartphone. Let's call him Bruno. The only tools at our disposal were SMS and phone calls, which are, by their very nature, slower mediums of communication. Our texting compatibility was way off. Bruno preferred to send lengthy messages once every few days, whereas I would rather ricochet between our favourite films and what we ate for lunch within a matter of minutes. But this is only my view in retrospect. At the time (and you can hear this on the podcast), I told listeners that I loved the fact that Bruno had a brick phone as opposed to a smart one. I smugly rattled off the list of benefits: 'We can really think about what we say to each other', 'It feels more real' and 'It's turning modern relationships on their head'. Like so many millennials, I fetishised authenticity. And for me, that meant rejecting modern technology in favour of something less advanced, as if that somehow rendered it more meaningful. It's only now that I realise I was probably only doing that as a form of self-preservation, one elicited after years of agonising over blue and grey ticks – and trying to convince myself that Bruno and I were a match when we so clearly were not.

It would have been okay if Bruno liked talking on the phone, but he didn't seem very interested in doing that either. The one phone call we had was stunted and awkward – and I'm pretty sure I could hear him typing on his computer while I spoke. But this is less than surprising. The advent of instant messaging platforms has meant that the humble phone call now seems archaic. Hence why millennials famously hate talking on the phone. This is well-documented – I don't know how many ways there are to write articles with the headline: 'Why millennials hate phone calls', but trust me, there are many.

A recent survey found that 75 per cent of millennials actively avoid phone calls because they're 'too time consuming'.* Meanwhile, another 81 per cent said they get apprehension anxiety before making a phone call. Again, this is all exacerbated when the person you're phoning is someone you fancy. I always used to think I loved phone calls. I would tell myself that I preferred them to instant messages because, again, they felt more authentic. I realised how drastically wrong I was when a gorgeous artist I'd been messaging for a few weeks decided to ring me one Saturday morning. We'd met a few times before but this was our first phone call. The phone chat had been coyly arranged under the playful guise of it being a

---

* BankMyCell spoke to more than 1,200 respondents aged between 22 and 37 years old in October 2018.

'therapy session' for him to talk me through a career hurdle. Our conversations had flowed thus far via text. Within just a few exchanges on WhatsApp, we seemed to have developed our own lexicon complete with codes and jokes that only we could understand. There was a major time difference (he was based in San Francisco) and so we would frequently speak while I was at work and he was about to go to sleep. I would repeatedly tell him to stop bothering me when it was quite obvious that I really wanted him to bother me all day.

Unfortunately, our rapport did not translate to a phone call. The minute he said 'hello', I realised how much I liked him and became paralysed by nerves. While he happily rambled on about what kind of alcohol he liked (rum) and what books he was reading (*The Course of Love* by Alain de Botton), I was too scared to say anything in case I sounded naive or ignorant, so bar the sporadic interjection of 'cool' and 'that's great', I actually said very little. There was one moment of silence between us, and so I immediately decided to fill it with something fabulously funny. Only I couldn't think of anything fast enough and somehow settled on something about driving lessons. Here I was thinking I was all superior and interested in 'real conversations', when in fact I was just another millennial cliché whose confidence was crippled by real-time interactions.

I spent days trying to work out what went wrong. Maybe I was socially inept. Maybe I just shouldn't talk to people on the phone. Or maybe this gorgeous artist was simply too gorgeous for me to maintain any semblance of normality on the phone to. I soon realised it was about control. When I was messaging the artist over text, even though I'd usually reply quickly, I had the option of taking a bit of time to mull over my messages. I could draft and redraft my witty replies fifty times if I wanted to. In other words, I had the luxury of being able to pause for thought, without having to endure an awkward five-minute-long silence. This was what I'd become accustomed to, so when it was taken away from me on the phone, I was at a bit of a loss.

Here's the caveat, though. If two people like each other, one awkward phone conversation is not game over. Of course, your first phone conversation with someone will have awkward moments. You're still getting to know each other. Working out each other's rhythms takes time. If he liked me, the artist would have called again, regardless of our awkward phone call. He would have found my driving lessons joke charming, rather than humiliating. And he would have thought it was sweet, maybe even flattering, that I was clearly feeling a bit shy.

A few months after that phone call, I slept with the artist. And that's when I started talking to people on the phone again.

When someone we like is not communicating in the way we expect or want them to, it makes us anxious. A lot of the issues I've described in this chapter would be eliminated if two people had the same texting styles and the same approach to phone calls. And yes, perhaps none of this would matter at all if the two people communicating liked each other the same amount. The issue is that when you are in the early stages of communicating with someone you fancy, you don't know what kind of communicator they are. You end up analysing every exchange you have like it's a university dissertation. You hold on to every comment and comma and use them to weave entire tapestries of someone's life story. You make mountains out of the most insignificant of molehills, like how a person uses semicolons, and whether they abbreviate words, and how many Xs they add when they say goodbye.

Behaving in this way doesn't mean you're strange, obsessive, or even desperate. It means you're normal. It means you're behaving in exactly the way that social media messaging platforms want you to. Why do you think they invented read receipts in the first place? By giving us access to this degree of detail, it keeps us hooked to our phones. It keeps us opening these apps regardless of whether or not we have a notification. Perhaps we are checking to see if those ticks have turned blue, or to check when someone was 'last active'. What these platforms have done is harness the power of social pressure in a way that makes us addicted to them. Coupled with infatuation, which is synonymous with obsession, it's no wonder we behave the way we do.

It's time we recognised this and went a little easier on ourselves. I know I've spent far too long punishing myself for agonising over those double blue ticks, or for sending a quadruple message, or for playing 'The Waiting Game'. This way of thinking breeds self-hatred. It makes us think we're mad or delusional for simply caring in a way we've been conditioned to. But it's okay to overthink something. And it's even better to feel things deeply. If we didn't, we wouldn't ever fall in love.

Chapter Three
#CoupleGoals

I have a problem with the term 'sliding into DMs'. The issue is not so much with the action itself (more on that later), but with the language. To slide is to slip. It is to skate. To skim. It implies your actions are smooth, subtle even. But when you think about what the term actually means, this makes no sense. Sliding into someone's DMs is the act of sending an unsolicited direct message on either Twitter or Instagram. But you're not venturing in there to discuss the weather or what you ate for breakfast. What defines a 'DM slide' in the traditional sense is the intent: you slide into someone's DMs because you want to fuck them – and there's nothing smooth or subtle about that.

A DM slide is a very unique form of communication. If you want to call someone, you call them. If you want to text someone, you text them. If you want to text or call someone whose number you don't have, that's when you slide into their DMs. This is why the DM slide is most often directed at people we admire from afar. It's the high school crushes we never got over. It's the colleagues we've made eyes at in the canteen. It's the celebrities we've had sex dreams about.

On Twitter, there are restrictions as to who you can DM; many accounts only accept private messages from their followers. These have recently been introduced on Instagram, too, but most people don't switch off their DM feature. This means that, generally speaking, anyone can message anyone, regardless of how many followers they have, or who they are. So yes, 'Hot Guy with the Blue Eyes' in the Accounts department has his DMs open, but so does Justin Timberlake. And Madonna. And Barack Obama. You can message them, and they can, in theory, message you back. When you DM someone who doesn't follow you, it appears in their 'message requests' folder, which the user has to 'accept' in order to reply. They can still read it, but you won't know this unless they accept it. Naturally, the more followers you have, the more message requests you receive and are therefore likely to ignore. Nonetheless, this has not stopped people from convincing themselves they have a chance with their celebrity crushes, particularly after a few glasses of wine. I put a call-out on Twitter for stories from people who had sent a flirty DM to a celebrity they fancied. Lots replied, with many specifying that they had been mildly intoxicated at the time. One sent this to George Ezra: 'Just wondering if I took you for a drink, what would you get?'. Another told Emily Ratajkowski they liked her nose. And one asked Ariana Grande if she'd 'like to go up the Shard'. None received a reply.

I wanted to know how common this was, so I asked the person I know with the most Instagram followers (470,000), my friend, the singer Ella Eyre. 'I receive around twenty DMs a day,' she told me. While the majority of these are from fans, some are from people who believe they are Eyre's soul mate. 'Can I take you out for dinner?', read one. 'Helloooooo', read another, which would have been harmless had it not succeeded five other messages saying 'hellooooo' and 'hii' and 'hey there'.

Another person sends her links to YouTube videos every other day and one, who calls her 'Ells', insists he's 'not a ladies man' and keeps trying to sell her doughnuts. 'I find it funny but also confusing,' she told me. 'I guess people just think they have nothing to lose.'

When I interviewed the influencer-turned-fitness entrepreneur Grace Beverley, who has one million Instagram followers, on the podcast, she described being propositioned via DM as 'part of the job'. 'As someone who has spent the majority of her adult life with a following and in a relationship, it's more something you laugh about. Like, "hey, guess who slid into my DMs today?"' Beverley added that this can sometimes make things difficult for her romantic partners. 'You have to be with someone who's really confident in themselves.' She explained that in the past, romantic partners have thought that because of the amount of people sliding into her DMs, she was keeping them as backups. So, Beverley's partners would do the same and started keeping backups themselves. 'If I'm dating [someone] and I'm saying I'm enjoying spending time with you, I'm not lying,' she said. 'I'm actively not lying, I don't have the time for that. But I think a lot of people, because of the position I'm in, assume that that's not the case.'

Here's the thing about DMs: there's something about them that makes people feel less inhibited by conventional social codes. You know, the codes that would prevent you from walking up to a celebrity you've never met and trying to sell them doughnuts. Or the kind that would make you think twice before flirting with a colleague you don't know well or a social media influencer you don't know at all. Sending a DM feels very private. And it is. Here you are, on a social media platform that is about communicating with people in a public space. But by sending a DM, you are choosing to do the opposite within that same space. It's like being at a dinner party and whispering in someone's ear as opposed to just talking normally to them. The implication is that your message is too intimate to be broadcasted, and because you have the safety of knowing no one else will hear it besides the recipient, it liberates the sender.

There is a psychological explanation to all this. Countless studies have proven that people behave differently in private and in public. Perhaps you're an introvert but you adopt the persona of an extrovert in certain situations, like at work, or when you're with a group of friends. Maybe you're a shy person but can summon the courage to deliver a presentation to a room full of your colleagues, so they'd have no clue what you're actually like. Similarly, you might slide into Justin Bieber's DMs and ask him on a date despite the fact that you wouldn't even dare tell your friends that you think he's attractive. The way we flip-flop between different personas is called 'free-trait behaviour', as coined by psychologist Brian Little of the University of Cambridge. The theory states that people can behave out of character when they are pursuing a meaningful 'personal project'. In other words, it means that people can behave in ways that are unusual for them if they believe doing so will result in some sort of personal gain. Some people are more likely to do this than others. 'One of the personality traits that is most relevant to this whole issue is that of self-monitoring,' Little told me. Self-monitoring is a concept first observed by American psychologist Mark Snyder, that defines how much people control the way they present themselves to others in social situations. For example, a high self-monitor will shape their interactions to meet the demands of the context.

They might tell people what they think they want to hear as opposed to simply saying what they think, which is how a low self-monitor behaves. 'If a high self-monitor sends an e-mail to an individual, for example, they would be frustrated if the recipient responds with a bunch of people in CC,' Little explained. They would be annoyed because they would have crafted that e-mail for the initial recipient's eyes only. This is why Little said that low self-monitors are less likely to slide into people's DMs. 'They are much more likely to publicly proclaim their beliefs with little nuance or sensitivity to the needs of specific others.'

As you might've guessed, I am a high self-monitor. And I suspect most millennials are, because we entered into our twenties and thirties alongside the advent of social media, which has literally given us the ability to control how we present ourselves to others, one Valencia-filtered snap at a time. I often catch myself just scrolling through my own Instagram profile, not necessarily out of narcissism, but out of a strange compulsion to see how I'm perceived by others. During moments of self-doubt, I find it oddly comforting to do this, as if seeing photos of myself with friends reminds me of the person I am. In my case, I prove Little's theory correct: I am a high self-monitor and I have slid into people's DMs with, shall we say, flirtatious intent.

But this level of intimacy – the one that can make you feel invincible because everything you say is shrouded in secrecy – warrants scrutiny, because while it can give us the confidence to DM a crush, famous or otherwise, it can also elicit more nefarious forms of behaviour. To examine this further, let's return to the advent of the phrase 'sliding into DMs'.

According to Google Trends, searches for these words

began in December 2013, shortly after Instagram introduced the feature. Twitter had its DM feature installed in 2006, though at that time, you could only send messages of 140 characters or less, the same as a Tweet. It wasn't until 2015 – two years after presumably seeing how Instagram had benefited from the feature – that Twitter allowed the sending of messages of any length. But back to Google. Online searches for 'sliding into DMs' had been climbing slowly since the end of 2013 until April 2014, when there was a major spike. That was the first time it became apparent that people were sliding into DMs for sex. I know what you're thinking, how could we possibly know such a thing? Well, the reason why we know such a thing is because of James Franco – and because the person whose DMs he slid into was 17 years old.

Lucy Clode was on holiday in New York with her mum and had gone to watch Franco in the Broadway production *Of Mice and Men*. The story goes that Franco, who was 35 at the time, had noticed the teenager taking selfies by the stage door as he was leaving the theatre and shouted for her to put the photos on Instagram and 'tag' him – a video of this exchange was published by a UK tabloid, as was the selfie of Franco and Clode. After Clode posted the photograph, Franco DM'd her. The conversation started with a simple 'Hi', to which Clode replied 'hi' alongside a shocked cat face emoji. What came next, according to screenshots obtained by the tabloids, makes for chilling reading.

James Franco: Where do you live?
Franco: NYC?
Lucy Clode: Scotland

Clode: In a small town called Dollar

Franco: How long will you be in New York?

Clode: Oops sorry, um, a few days it's my 18th birthday present.

Franco: You're 18?

Franco: Who are you with?

Franco: Do you have a bf?

Clode: Nearly 18, my mum and not if you're around.

Franco: When is your bday?

Franco: Where are you staying?

Franco: What's your #?

Clode: In May but I have exams then just off of Times Square in a Hilton, what you mean #?

The next screenshots of the duo's conversation appears to be in iMessage.

Franco: Can I see you?

Clode: As long as you are james Franco

Franco: I am

Franco: You're single?

Franco: What's the hotel?

Franco: Should I rent a room?

Clode: April fools was an hour ago though . . . [sic]

Franco sends Clode a selfie of himself waving.

Franco: It's me

Franco: Yes or no?

Franco: Tomorrow or Thurs?

Franco: Ok. Be well

Franco: X

Clode: I'll come back when I'm 18

Franco: X

Clode: Well this is a story my Scottish friends will never
   believe

Franco: Don't tell

Clode: I just want proper evidence that it's you and I won't

Franco: I gave it to you. If you don't want to meet, then
   text me when you do. Bye.

Clode: You sound so dodgy though

Franco: Bye

Clode: One second, I will meet you if you write my name
   on a piece of paper then send it to me with your face
   also in the picture please

Franco replied with a selfie of himself holding a piece of paper
with the word 'Lucy' scrawled across it.

As far as we know, Clode and Franco never did meet –
though neither replied to my requests for comment to confirm
this. But the exchange prompted worldwide media coverage,
resulting in Franco ultimately confessing he felt 'embarrassed'
about the whole ordeal. 'It's the way that people meet each
other today, but what I've learned – I guess because I'm new
to it – is you don't know who's on the other end,' he said on
the US talk show, *Live with Kelly and Michael*. 'You get a feel
for them, you don't know who you're talking to. I used bad
judgement and I learned my lesson. But unfortunately in my
position, I mean I have a very good life, but not only do I
have to go through the embarrassing rituals of meeting
someone, sometimes if I do that, then it gets published for
the world so now it's doubly embarrassing.'

Revisiting this story today is jarring for more reasons than
one, and how it was handled says a lot about how much
society has progressed in terms of holding predatory men to

account. In that clip, Kelly, Michael and the entire audience laugh along with Franco as he makes his statement. Not only do they accept what he says without questioning it, they actually sympathise with him. What's more, Kelly tells Franco that 'it happens to everybody', making it seem like an adult hitting on a teenager is akin to taking a tumble on the street.

But let's focus on Franco's excuse. Speaking to Kelly and Michael, he doesn't apologise – or even acknowledge – his predation, or the fact that Clode was 17 years old. Instead, his reaction comes across like this: 'I got it wrong, but it wasn't my fault. It's Instagram's fault. I know I'm a Hollywood celebrity, but I'm also just a regular guy who wants to meet someone and fall in love. This is how it's done today, so I had a stab at it. Now everyone knows about it and I'm embarrassed. Pity me.' All this is apparently enough to convince Michael, Kelly and the rapturously applauding audience that Franco deserves our forgiveness. So complex is the world of dating on social media, it can vindicate a man for allegedly trying to sleep with an underage girl. Or at least it could then.

I highly doubt you'd see a conversation like that on TV now, but Franco's hopeless defence illustrates an important point: sliding into someone's DMs can backfire, particularly if you have the ego of a Hollywood movie star and you fail to pick up on very obvious textual cues. Let's put the age gap aside for a moment (it's hard to factor that in without having a very different discussion) and imagine these were two adults of the same age. The conversation that Franco has with Clode would still be the perfect example of what not to do when you slide into someone's DMs. Firstly, aside from Franco yelling 'tag me' at Clode after they took a selfie together, the duo had no previous interactions prior to messaging privately. That is an immediate red flag because it makes Franco's message feel presumptuous. Had the two previously commented on each other's posts, followed one another, or had a conversation in real life, his DM slide might have seemed more organic. Then there is Franco's first message: 'where do you live?'. Remember, we're on Instagram here, the place where people have usernames like 'Camille's Closet' and 'Silver Shiny Things'. It's not the norm to share your surname, let alone your address. Franco then dives into an intense line of questioning, with one nosy (and predatory) thought after another. Even if he wasn't asking very forward questions – such as, 'do you have a bf' – the fact that he sends multiple messages, asks one question after another and continues even when Clode replies just once reflects a clear imbalance. To anyone else, Clode's short and polite replies would imply disinterest. The other person would take the hint and stop trying. But Franco persists.

The thing about sliding into someone's DMs is that you have to be tacit and tactful, particularly if this is someone you don't know well or have never met. By sliding in uninvited, so to speak, you are already imposing. It's therefore crucial to be respectful if it's obvious that the person is not matching your interest. This matters far more on Instagram than on a dating app. On most apps, you have to 'match' with someone before you can send them a message. Also, you're on a dating app, so your intentions are clear: you're there to meet someone. On Instagram, you don't have to match with anyone before you can message them. And you're essentially just there to share photos, which can make matters slightly murkier.

This brings me to a specific form of sliding into someone's

DMs known as 'Tindstagramming', a harmful dating trend that was first reported about in 2017. This is how it works: someone who you've rejected on a dating app finds you on Instagram and slides into your DMs to give it another shot. Tindstagramming became easier in 2015, when Tinder allowed users to link their Instagram accounts to the app. Judging from everything that has been written about Tindstagramming online and from the messages I've received, it is most commonly something that men do to women. In such instances, the implication is that when a woman rejects a man on a dating app, she doesn't mean 'no', what she really means is 'try harder'. It's ideologies like these that are held among incels, or 'involuntary celibates', a dangerous internet subculture of men who view sex as something that women 'owe' them. Their beliefs are rooted in misogyny, violence and specifically, violence against women. In other words, Tindstagramming is not just another kitschy dating trend – it's something we should take very seriously indeed.

To give you an idea of the kind of messages people send when they are Tindstagramming, here are some taken from screenshots that women have shared on Twitter.

Found you on Tinder cutie, how are you? And I like feet too

Hello, we didn't match on Tinder so I'm awkwardly attempting to stalk you on ig. It looks like you're kinda into awkward

How are you? I saw your profile on Tinder and I wanted to drop you a line to say hello.

Hey what's good! I saw you on Tinder. Wyd tonight?

One woman, let's call her Bella, shared her stories of Tindstagramming with me – she had two. The first person was someone Bella had accidentally swiped right on while using a dating app. 'I had the flu and was in a state of high fever, so I was not thinking straight,' she said. After this user's messages to Bella went ignored, he slid into her Instagram DMs. 'It turned out he sort of worked in the same industry as me and we knew loads of people in common. At that stage I thought, "Oh maybe it's worth a punt even though he doesn't seem like my type and also it will be impolite now if I don't agree to a date".' They went on one date – he could not stop talking about himself and his 'crazy' ex. 'That was enough to put me off, but he did keep trying,' Bella added.

The second man DM'd Bella after having seen her on Bumble – she had not swiped right. 'I'm not a stalker, promise . . .' was his opening line. 'That should have been warning enough,' Bella recalled. He asked her out, but she was also unwell at the time. 'Then he started sending me hand-sketched get well soon cards. Like . . . a lot of them. I couldn't work out whether it was sweet or odd.' Eventually, they met up. 'There was zero chemistry. Part of what I'd liked about him was that he seemed to have a decent, normal job and the first thing he did when we met was tell me he'd jacked it all in and spent his life savings on producing and performing his own album of soft rock.' The evening came to an end, she dodged the kiss. The next day, he texted her to say he had written a song for her. 'I was SO cringed out, I never replied. It's the only time I've ever ghosted someone and I feel really bad about it but also I felt sick.'

None of this is Instagram's fault. Nor is it Tinder's fault. And it certainly isn't Bella's fault, or that of anyone else who has been a victim of Tindstagramming. And who knows, for some people, this approach might lead to a loving relationship. But that doesn't make it okay that people are exploiting the pitfalls of modern technology to pursue those that have already rejected them. Just because you can message anyone on Instagram, does not mean that you should. And there are ways to slide into someone's DMs and not come across as creepy, predatory, or invasive. Ample celebrity couples have started this way. To name but a few: Ricky Martin and Jwan Yosef; Dua Lipa and Anwar Hadid; Sarah Hyland and Wells Adams; Nick Jonas and Priyanka Chopra; Joe Jonas and Sophie Turner. All these couples had some sort of prior exchange either in real life or on Instagram before venturing into the DMs. Lipa and Hadid met at a barbecue. Turner and Jonas had been told they'd get along by mutual friends. And Hyland and Adams were already flirting publicly on Twitter when Adams slid into her DMs to suggest they meet for tacos. 'I was single, obviously, and was like, "This is really awesome. You're being very forward and it's sexy and not aggressive, but very confident and sexy," and I liked that,' Hyland recalled in an interview.

You don't have to have oodles of followers to fall in love over a DM, either. Many people with modest followings – i.e. non-famous people – have gone on to have happy relationships after having slid into one another's DMs. When I tweeted a request to speak to people who had met this way, I received more than twenty replies, including one from a woman named Ashley. She actually married someone who slid into her Twitter DMs to ask about a photograph of a cheesecake she'd posted. 'It was under the guise of us forming a London Cheesecake Club,' she told me. 'He wrote a manifesto for it and everything.

He was stuck in a car with his family on a five-hour drive, so we exchanged flirty food-themed chat for several hours. Within three days we'd arranged our first date. That was eight years ago – we've been married for five years now and have a toddler. We both still love cheesecake, though curiously, the London Cheesecake Club never really took off. The manifesto is framed on our bathroom wall.'

This has also happened to me, though my story is not quite as sweet. I met Joe at work – ironically, when I was recording an episode of *Millennial Love*. He worked on the video team and had stepped in to help produce the episode because our regular producer was off that day. My then co-host, Rachel, asked if we'd met before. I said we hadn't and Joe came over to shake my hand. He was tall, socially awkward and wearing a black graphic T-shirt, all of which was enough for me to convince myself that he was Seth Cohen reincarnate. I thought he was ridiculously hot. I followed Joe on Twitter the next day and squealed in the office when I saw the notification that he had followed me back. The next few days revolved around me punctiliously planning my outfits for work. I wore the jeans that made my legs look great and the white T-shirt that hung loosely enough off my shoulders to reveal my black bra strap. I also spent time scrupulously planning a 'work drinks' at the pub – I hoped someone else would invite Joe so I could pretend this was not all my idea. Thankfully, they did, and we spent the evening chatting giddily about northern California and our mutual fascination with Silicon Valley bosses who've banned their kids from using social media. It took him three days to slide into my DMs (Twitter, not Instagram). I was making cupcakes in my kitchen when I saw his message: a 'hey!' that was noticeably all lower-case. Within a few minutes, we were off. Books, podcasts, everything we loved and didn't love about our jobs. There was a lot to talk about. Eventually, he asked if I wanted to 'hang out'. I did. Though that initial ambiguity should've been a clear indicator that Joe and I would not 'hang out' for long.

Side note: I have a major issue with the phrase 'hang out'. As I mentioned in Chapter One, it is textbook Fuck Boy language. By using this term – and refraining from ever using more conventional words like 'date', 'partner', or 'girlfriend' – it absolves the user of responsibility when, later, they behave badly or decide to call things quits without giving a proper explanation. If this upsets you, they will say: 'Oh, I didn't think we were even dating.' Or worse: 'I thought we were just hanging out?'.

After three months, Joe ended it. I can't quite call it a break-up because when I asked the fateful 'what are we?' question six weeks in, Joe made it very clear that we were not boyfriend and girlfriend and never would be. *He only wanted to hang out.* But the actual point here is that it was the dissolution of my unidentifiable relationship with Joe that led me to post my first thirst trap.

A thirst trap is 'an action, image, or statement designed to solicit sexual attention'. At least, that's what it says in the Collins Dictionary. In fact, a thirst trap is much more complex than that. Look at the language. 'Thirst', drawing on the phrase: 'thirsting for attention', implying desire. 'Trap' adds an element of manipulation, making it sound as if you're posting a photo as a means of luring your crush into a trapdoor above your bed.

It's not entirely clear who came up with the term. According to Google Trends, people started searching for the phrase in

2013, and search interest has steadily increased ever since. It took until 2014 for the first '25 Instagram #ThirstTraps Set By Celebrities We Happily Stepped Into' round-up to be born, and there's been a pretty regular flow of thirst traps, and articles about them, ever since. But none quite compare to those about Demi Lovato, whose meticulous thirst trap strategy went viral in January 2018. It was focused. It was smart. It was, dare I say, a work of art.

This was back in the day when Instagram still had its 'following activity' page, which allowed you to see what posts the people you followed had liked and commented on. According to the multiple screenshots of Lovato's activity – shared across the internet, notably by YouTuber Tyler Oakley – her game plan went something like this. She identified her target: the actor Henry Cavill. Then, she liked two of Cavill's most recent posts. Next came the 'trap': a photograph of Lovato wearing white lingerie and staring straight down the lens. Then – and here comes the crucial part of how the thirst trap works – she *followed* Cavill. Genius, isn't it? It worked, too. Because Cavill, who already followed Lovato, proceeded to like some of her posts. He even commented on one: 'This is awesome! Nice one Miss Lovato!' Everyone knows that despite being archaic and a little bit sexist, putting 'Miss' in front of someone's surname sounds flirty. So, despite the fact that Cavill and Lovato never dated (as far as we know), we can assume that Lovato's strategy was a success, because at the very least, it got Cavill to notice her.

It's rare for someone to identify their own thirst trap as a thirst trap. For example, Lovato's post was not captioned: 'this is a thirst trap'. The caption was: 'Big news coming soon'. The idea is that only the person posting knows it's a thirst trap because, as with everything else in dating, your intentions are supposed to be ambiguous, even when they couldn't be more obvious. 'Oh, I just happened to be wearing sexy underwear when someone just happened to walk into the room and take a photo of me looking really hot. Then, I just happened to post it on Instagram. Oh, the person I fancy might see it? Cool. Not sure how that happened.'

We adopt this guise of serendipity a lot on social media, but particularly so when we're trying to catch someone's attention. It forms part of the shame that we attach to vanity: it's uncool to share a photograph of yourself looking good, and it's very uncool to share one in the hope that other people will think you look good. This is especially true for women, who are almost always more likely than men to be labelled 'desperate' for posting a thirst trap and are more likely to be judged harshly for posting a nice photograph of themselves. Hence why the 'Challenge Accepted' Instagram trend that surfaced in the summer of 2020 was so galling. The campaign purported to be about female empowerment and 'women supporting women', but all it seemed to consist of – and require you to do – was post a black and white photograph of yourself looking really hot.* It was like women had finally been given the green light to share a good photo of themselves without judgement. And the way they leapt at the opportunity (to date, the hashtag has more than six million posts) without even questioning where the hashtag came from, or what it

---

* Reports that the challenge originated from a bid to raise awareness about femicide in Turkey were quashed by *The New York Times*. In fact, the Challenge Accepted hashtag has been used since 2016 as a way of promoting female empowerment but bizarrely has never encouraged any form of donation or activism.

was even supporting . . . well, there's absolutely nothing empowering about that.

That's why it's always so refreshing when women post thirst traps and identify them as such. In December 2019, Kylie Jenner posted a black and white photograph of herself wearing lacy underwear in bed above the caption: 'Just didn't feel right going into 2020 without one last thirst trap.' Jenner had recently split from her ex, Travis Scott, leading her two hundred million followers to suspect that her 'trap' was aimed at him. Maybe it was, but maybe, *just maybe*, it was for herself.

It's understandable why people would want to post a thirst trap in the wake of a break-up. You might not be trying to 'trap' your ex, per se; you might just be in need of a self-esteem boost and posting a hot photo of yourself on Instagram is a quick-fix solution. That's why I posted mine. It was a few weeks after Joe dumped me; I was feeling particularly terrible about myself and in dire need of some validation. I wasn't ready to start dating other people, I just really needed someone to tell me I was hot. So, I found an old photograph of myself on holiday wearing an Agent Provocateur swimsuit that revealed the modest amount of cleavage I have. I posted it with Joe in mind – the caption might as well have been 'HA! LOOK AT WHAT YOU'RE MISSING!' – but, really, that picture was for me. And when the likes rolled in – 155, to be specific – I really did feel a boost of self-confidence and for a moment, forgot that the person I'd spent weeks obsessing over found me undesirable. Because if 155 people 'liked me' online, maybe someone else would eventually like me in real life again.

When my ex-boyfriend and I got together, one of the things I told him very early on was that I had a strict policy against sharing our relationship on Instagram. 'It's embarrassing, it's unnecessary and literally no one cares,' I told him, rather smugly. I did not want to be one of *those* couples. You know, the kind that use a self-timer to take photos of themselves snogging aggressively in loungewear or write sycophantic captions about 'this one' smiling next to a £10 plate of avocado toast. I wince at those posts. And they're all eerily similar. Search #CoupleGoals on Instagram and you'll find millions of near-identical shots of straight, white couples in some sort of highly Instagrammable scenario: think sipping cocktails at sunset/doing acro-yoga/eating brunch. The hashtag implies that this is what an ideal relationship looks like. But does anyone actually straddle their partner on a public beach and lick their face off? Who actually wants to share a bubble bath? And who is the poor third wheel that's been bribed/hired to take all these photos?

I posed these questions (more politely, of course) to one of Instagram's most beloved couples, Oliver Proudlock and Emma Louise Connolly, who have since got married. They are quite literally the definition of #CoupleGoals to the point where they even have their own hashtag, #opxec, which contains more than 1,600 posts of them looking so absurdly into each other that they could almost be satirical. Proudlock and Connolly have well over one million followers between them, including a couple of hundred thousand on their @casaproudlock account, which is dedicated to sharing pictures of their devastatingly plush London townhouse. The majority of their couple snaps are taken by their joint publicist, but when she's not around, Connolly told me she has a talent for creating a tripod out of anything.

Given my stance on couples like this, I was expecting to find Proudlock and Connolly rather irritating. But the second these two happy shiny people walked into the studio to record an episode of the podcast, I – like all their followers – fell hopelessly in love with them. They were friendly, polite and held hands under the table throughout our recording. The whole thing was quite saccharine, but it warmed my icy heart.

'I think people like to see love,' Connolly said when I asked what it is about their content that resonates with people. 'We put selective parts of our relationship online that people get to see and feel a part of. People just like to see people happy.' At this point, Proudlock chimed in to point out that since their relationship began five years ago they have both shared parts of their relationship on Instagram, so their followers have 'been on a journey' with them. The former *Made in Chelsea* star said, 'I think with anything that you're sharing, whether it's love or your day-to-day life, authenticity is one of the most important things,' he added. I know what you're thinking: which part of doing acro-yoga on the beach at sunset while your publicist scrambles to take the perfect photo is authentic? But Proudlock and Connolly won't just post the final shot, they'll also post the messy, clumsy behind-the-scenes photos that were taken to get that one winning post. I'm still not entirely convinced that counts as authentic. On a platform that is predicated on inauthenticity – with filters, editing tools that allow you to literally edit the way people see your life – is it even possible to be authentic?

I posed this question to illustrator and former podcast guest Flo Perry. She told me that she's suspicious of couples who post excessively about their relationship. 'I think you're more likely to post gushing public declarations of love on your Instagram if that love feels fragile. It makes sense, because seeing the likes roll in on a "couple photo" can temporarily make you feel more secure that you're doing the right thing in staying together. When your love feels secure, however, you don't need those public declarations of love to feel loved. You feel loved every day in the offline world.'

This is definitely not the case with Proudlock and Connolly – I refuse to believe that anyone could fake that kind of adoration – but it certainly is for some couples, who might see sharing their relationship online as a way of glazing over its real-life cracks. As the comments and likes roll in on their cute couple snaps, with people gushing that they are 'perfect for each other', they might start to believe it themselves. This is toxic for several reasons; one of which being that it can also keep you in a relationship for longer than you should be. This was the case for Grace Beverley, who used to share a lot of her relationship with an ex-boyfriend on her social media. They would star in YouTube videos together, do Q and As, and regularly post Instagram Stories about one another.

'I've had a social media relationship before, and it's all lies,' she said when she came on the podcast. 'Like, you're never going to put an argument on social media [. . .] it wasn't even intentionally fabricating anything it was just, like, that is not representative of how I felt at that moment and I think it creates this, even as a moral responsibility as an influencer, it creates this completely incorrect idea of what a relationship was. And the picture of that relationship was just completely inaccurate.' The issue for Beverley, she said, was that because she and her ex created content together, she convinced herself that their relationship had become a part of her job. And this meant she stayed in that relationship for much longer than she should have.

Beverley took a completely different approach to her next

relationship. 'I posted a photo once or twice and sometimes on my Story. But I was never in a video, never anything like that.' This strategy helped a lot when Beverley and this partner broke up, because none of her followers knew about it and so weren't able to comment on it. This was a refreshing change from her last break-up, when Beverley's followers would regularly offer their thoughts on her relationship and the dynamic between her and her then-partner. 'I was like, "well maybe [the comments were] useful because it made us realise things we wouldn't have necessarily realised" and then I thought, actually no. I don't think there was one useful bit of input from an outside party. Because for anyone whose opinion should matter, I'll be able to contact them directly. Or they'll be able to contact me directly.'

Listening to Beverley, I was fascinated by the extent to which her followers were so invested in her love life that they felt compelled to police it. While everyone is of course entitled to their own opinion, forming one about another person's relationship is quite a leap – particularly if you don't even know that person. No one really knows what is going on within a relationship apart from the people in that relationship. And yet we *love* to pass judgements on relationships we aren't a part of, whether they're those of our friends, our family members, or of the influencers and celebrities we follow on Instagram. What's more, we love to compare them to our own, as we do with almost everything on social media. There's a sense of *schadenfreude* when you witness another relationship falling apart, as if it somehow validates your own. This way of thinking turns relationships into a kind of competitive sport, one that rewards so-called happy couples and punishes unhappy ones, or worse, single people – remember when

Bridget Jones is made to feel a social leper at a dinner with all her married friends? As the essayist Tim Kreider put it, 'we're all anxiously sizing up how everyone else's decisions have worked out to reassure ourselves that our own are vindicated – that we are, in some sense, winning'.*

Hence why sharing your relationship on social media is such an interesting phenomenon, because it invites commentary that no one is really at liberty to give. This is more pertinent for someone in Beverley's position, of course. In the wake of her recent break-up, she explained how her followers would approach her on the street or DM her to let her know that they'd seen her ex-boyfriend with another woman. 'I've had multiple times where people have been like, "hey just to let you know I think your boyfriend might be cheating on you because I just saw him with this person". And I'm like, "well thanks we broke up!"'

Beverley's followers don't just approach her when they think something is up with her relationship, they approach her partners, too. 'My ex, for example, was once working and he was talking to one of his colleagues and someone came up to him and was like, "Hope you're keeping this savoury, I know you're Grace Beverley's boyfriend." And he was like, "this is my colleague!"'

The difficulty for people like me, who insist that they are averse to sharing photos of their relationship online, is that couple photos have become so normalised on Instagram – there are currently more than thirty million posts under #CoupleGoals – it's impossible to ignore them. Even if they aren't all the

---

* *The New York Times*, 2009, The Referendum.

schmaltzy all-over-each-other kind of posts, they're still there, infiltrating your Instagram feed. Seeing these posts on a regular basis fosters a 'pics or it didn't happen' culture. It's not so much that if you don't post about your relationship, people will question if you're in one – it's more that refraining from posting about your relationship implies that you are withholding something. A flaw, perhaps, or some kind of deep-rooted unhappiness in that relationship. And that can breed serious insecurities within your relationship if, say, your partner actively refuses to post about you.

A few weeks after I'd firmly imposed a no-Instagram rule on my boyfriend, which he duly obliged, I started noticing how he'd used Instagram in his previous relationships. And it was quite a lot. There were photos of his ex-girlfriends on trips abroad, having fun at festivals, or sitting across from him at the dinner table. There was even a post to mark a one-year anniversary of a previous relationship. Seeing how visible his ex-partners were on his Instagram feed made me feel like I was somehow invisible, despite the fact that I felt secure in our relationship. In the end, I asked him to post something about us – and he did, on his Instagram Story.

As petty as it may sound, there's a major difference between posting about someone on your Instagram Story, where it will stay for just twenty-four hours, and posting about them on your main feed, or on your 'grid', as it's often called. In many ways, whether you choose to post about someone on your Story versus your Grid is a sign of commitment. It's transience versus permanence. It's fast food versus a Michelin starred meal. It's someone you're sleeping with versus someone you're in love with. When you post about a partner on your grid, it renders your relationship 'Instagram Official' – see the countless tabloid articles using the term in reference to the celebrity couples who have done this. When you post about someone on your Story, it's apropos of nothing. Which is why I was really annoyed when, nine months into our relationship, my boyfriend still hadn't posted a picture of me on his grid. Let me point out some of the basic hypocrisies here that make this completely ridiculous. One: I was the person who had initially told him not to post anything specifically about our relationship. Two: I was the one who had previously been adamant that I did not want to become a couple who shares photos of their relationship on Instagram. Three: in light of all of this, I had suddenly decided that if my boyfriend did not post about our relationship, it meant that he didn't love me, despite the fact that I hadn't shared a single post or Story about him.

I'm not the only person who has these thoughts. 'I've definitely said the words: "Why do you never post about me on your Instagram?"', Perry told me. 'When you see other couples constantly posting appreciation posts for their partner, if your partner doesn't do that, it can feel like they're not proud of you, or that they don't feel the urge to show you off. But that probably isn't the case. They probably don't feel the need to shout about how much they love you because they are telling you so often in other ways. They're hopefully too busy staring into your eyes to get their phone out to post a picture of you. Don't get me wrong, the occasional public declaration of love is amazing, and I want to feature on my girlfriend's grid because I don't want all those other bitches getting the wrong idea and thinking she's single. But more Instas doesn't necessarily mean more love.'

I still wonder how I could have been so irritated by something that is essentially completely meaningless. What difference does it make if my boyfriend shares a photograph of me at all, let alone whether it's on Stories or the Grid? Why should it matter? The answer is that it really shouldn't, but unfortunately, in a society where social media is viewed as a metric of success for everything from your career to your relationship, it does matter. It matters quite a lot.

Just as it has become common practice to share photos of your relationship on Instagram, it has become just as common to delete them when that relationship comes to an end. We hear about celebrities doing this all the time in the tabloids: 'XX DELETES ALL EVIDENCE OF RELATIONSHIP WITH YY AND UNFOLLOWS THEIR SISTER' – spare a thought for the intern whose job it is to trawl through celebrity Instagram accounts to uncover that information. I asked Proudlock and Connolly what they thought about this on the podcast. Is it a little extreme? Or is it a necessary part of ending a modern day relationship? In other words, what is the correct post-break-up Instagram etiquette?

'It's so relative to the person,' said Connolly, who has removed every post related to past relationships from her Instagram. 'It's just like a fresh start, I think. Although it's savage. But I think you kind of owe that to yourself to be able to wipe the slate clean if you want to.' Proudlock concurred that whether or not you delete posts featuring an ex very much depends on the circumstances with which that relationship ended. 'If it was a really full-on break-up, and reminders of it is really having a negative effect and you need to have that clean slate, then I think you have to delete.'

I've always thought it was a bit much to remove the remnants of a past relationship on Instagram. Your past is your past – you can't just 'delete' a relationship. At least, you can't delete it for yourself. But by removing the photos from your Instagram account, you can sort of delete it for your followers, who will no longer have access to those photos. For them, and those who browse your profile, it will be like it never existed. I can see why there'd be some comfort in that, particularly if, as Proudlock and Connolly said, the relationship has ended badly. In which case, deleting those posts could be the very thing that allows you to move on. It is the contemporary version of throwing old photos in the fire and sighing in relief as you watch them burn.

I never posted a photograph of Joe and I on Instagram, so there was nothing to delete. But trust me, if I had, those posts would be long gone by now. As Proudlock and Connolly say though, context is key. I would have deleted any posts featuring Joe because that break-up (if you can even call it that) had a major impact on my self-esteem. Keeping any remnants of him on my feed would have been like a form of self-harm, serving only to remind me of how awful he made me feel.

It was a different matter altogether when it came to photos of my ex-boyfriend – the one who did eventually start sharing photos of me on his Grid and, understandably, encouraged me to follow suit. So, I posted photos too. Several, in fact. And even though we've since broken up, I've kept them there, because I have finally begun to understand that there's another reason why people share photos of their relationship on Instagram. And it has nothing to do with seeking validation or wanting to show it off. It's so that you can remember what it feels like to have been so in love with someone, that you wanted to tell a lot of other people about it. Maybe you wanted to shout about it from the rooftops or jump up and down on Oprah's couch on live TV, as Tom Cruise famously did when he declared his love to his then-girlfriend Katie Holmes in 2005. But you couldn't do either of those things, so you posted it on Instagram instead. That, I understand. Because as I write this, I'm single. And so that's the other reason why I'm looking back at old posts of me and my ex more than I'd care to admit. It's partly in the hope that I will love someone in that same way again. But mainly it's because I hope someone will love *me* like that again. I feel proud that someone once did – and that's not a feeling I'm ready to delete just yet.

Chapter Four
Information Overload

'I just need a first name and the colour of his hair. Give me twenty minutes.' That was the response from my friend, Molly, when I told her I'd met a hot guy on a catering shift and wanted to find him on social media. I was 21 at the time and working part time as a waitress for an events company.

It had been a particularly dry spell for my love life – the most heated exchange I'd had in ten months was with my dentist over a botched filling – so when I met Alex, and we flirted over foie gras, I was determined not to let this just be another of those 'I met a hot guy and nothing happened' stories. This had to be an 'I met a hot guy and then *something happened*' kind of story. The problem was that Alex and I did not exchange numbers. And aside from the fact that he was a terrible waiter, the only tangible thing I knew about him was that he was an actor and he had thick brown hair, so he probably always ate his greens.

The events company I worked for was hideously old-fashioned. It was the kind of company that forced its female employees to wear big heels and small dresses. We even had our hair and makeup done. As for the events themselves, well. It was brunch with Ed Sheeran at Elton John's house. Canapés with Kate Moss at the V&A summer party. And drinks with

Eddie Redmayne inside Kensington Palace. These were Gatsby-worthy bashes: opulent, extravagant and populated by the upper echelons of British society. My point is that the staff had to match up. Most were models and actors – I'd wangled my way in through a friend – and had faces and bodies that looked as if they had been plucked from a Hollywood romcom and put through a Valencia filter. They were the kind of people that belonged in every room, even if they were working in it. I was always too intimidated to speak to any of them.

But then, Alex and I were paired together to work a birthday party in a ritzy London hotel. I would hold the canapés; he would pour the champagne. I fancied him so much, which unfortunately meant that I was so terrified I'd say something foolish or suddenly burst into a fit of nervous hiccups that I didn't say much at all during that shift. Thankfully, Alex was chatty enough to rattle on for hours. He told me about his burgeoning acting career, the Lynx advert he had once starred in, and how bizarre he thought it was that I had to wear high heels. I soon relaxed. Our chat wasn't overly flirty, but there was definitely a spark. I liked how he held eye contact with me when I spoke, despite how unnerving it was. It made me feel like he really wanted to hear what I had to say.

A few days passed and Alex was still very much on my mind. What if this was my meet-cute? What if this was the moment that would lead to a euphoric sex-filled marriage? And the spawning of several chiselled children? I had to find out. For help, I rang Molly, a self-identifying 'expert' in social media stalking. As promised, within twenty minutes of giving her the intel she needed, along with several alternative spellings of 'Alex' just in case (Alyx, Alix, Alicx), she sent me a text with links to Alex's Facebook profile and to the Lynx advert. I was both impressed and concerned. It's not as if Molly was an intelligence officer at MI6; she was an accountant at PWC. How had she found him? 'Please, it's sooo easy to find people online now,' she replied when I asked. 'I could've found him faster but he's not on Instagram.'

I tried not to think too much about what lengths Molly had gone to in order to obtain this information and added Alex as a friend. He'd recognise me immediately, accept my request and then message to ask me how I'd been. We'd exchange a few jokes about the catering company, how we felt guilty for working there given our feminist values, and then, after a few more hours of flirtatious back and forth, he'd ask me out. But of course, Alex did not accept my friend request. In fact, I'm fairly certain he rejected it and blocked me because I can't even find his profile anymore. My guess is that he saw my friend request and recoiled at the fact I'd found him on Facebook with so little information. At least, that is a kinder reality for me to accept than the more likely fact that he probably just didn't fancy me.

Nonetheless, the story is an important one, because it illustrates how easy it is to find the people we like online, even if they're a complete stranger. Before enlisting Molly's help, I'd tried finding Alex myself. I'd never done this before, so I started somewhat naively by Googling 'Alex actor London'. There were quite a few results. Most were for Alex Pettyfer, the British actor known for playing vacant floppy-haired guys in films such as *Magic Mike* and *Wild Child*. I tried searching the same on Twitter and Instagram to no avail. A similar failure on Facebook.

I went back to Molly. 'You met him in London, right? So,

let's assume that's where he's from. Go onto Facebook. Type in "Alex". Now, filter your results. Click "people". Then, where it says city, type "London". And in work, type "actor". Add everything else you know about him. You'd be surprised at how few people there are with those details.' I did what she said and while I was met with hundreds of profiles, it only took five minutes of scrolling to spot Alex's. There he was, surname and all. I browsed through profile photos that went as far back as 2007, I found out where he went to school, I saw which pubs he hung out at. All this information was mine for the taking, and yet, I felt incredibly uncomfortable taking it. Despite the fact that we'd met and, at least in my opinion, clicked, we hadn't actually exchanged details. I was far too shy to offer mine, but I suspect he wouldn't have been had he actually been interested in me. So, there I was, uncovering all this intel about a man who didn't fancy me and had no idea I even knew his last name. I was officially a creep.

The fact that all we need is a person's first name and hair colour to find them on social media is disconcerting. But that's the least of it. When I asked my Twitter followers about their social media stalking methods, their tactics read like something out of a John le Carré novel. Everyone had their own strategy depending on what information was available to them and how adept they were with the nuances of modern technology. And it transpires that if you are very adept, you may not even need a person's first name to find them online.

Social media stalking confessions from my Twitter inbox #1
– Anonymous woman, early twenties
So I went clubbing last year and met a girl but didn't get her name. I was SO into her. A few weeks passed and I saw

*that the club posted photos from the night out. I saw her
in one but only her friend was tagged. So I then went
through her friend's Friend list to find her. Eventually I did,
but I waited a while to reach out. When I reached out
months later (because life got busy), she was in Cambridge
where I was for one night only. We went on a date and it
went well. Unfortunately, we went on a second date and
we didn't click as much. I felt like SUCH a stalker for tracking
her down.*

It surprised me how many people said their preferred platform
for social media stalking was LinkedIn. You mean, the place
where people lie about how many languages they speak and
brag about getting an A* in GCSE maths? *That's* where you
go looking for love? The thing about LinkedIn, I've realised,
is that, of all the social media platforms, it has the most
in-depth search tool. You can enter all sorts of random information you might have on a person, such as which university
they went to, which sector they work in, where they've worked
previously, and where they're based. Then, once you've identified them, you can unearth even more intel. Like where they
went to school, what they scored in their A levels, and which
Thai animal shelter they once stroked sedated tigers at. All of
which is of course very relevant to whether you'll want to shag
them, apparently.

Another niche strategy I was told about is reverse searching photos on Google images. This very complicated-sounding
tactic was a firm favourite among some of my friends, including
one who confessed that it was her preferred method when she
was single. 'It's particularly useful if you met on a night out
and the club has posted photos on Facebook or Instagram,'

she told me. 'All you have to do is screenshot the photograph, cropping the person you're looking for if possible, then go to Google Images, click "Search by image". Upload the image of your crush and Google will show you "visually similar images", which could either bring up their celebrity doppel-gänger, or another photo of them from elsewhere on the internet that has their name attached.' For example, you could reverse search a club snap of someone and then Google would serve up their LinkedIn profile photo, or their Instagram handle, and possibly their full name.

We go to extreme lengths to find out more about the people we fancy. And while it's easy to poke fun, there is clearly a darker undercurrent to all this. Once you have a person's full name, you can dive headfirst into the rabbit hole of their online persona. You can look them up on Instagram, Facebook, Twitter, maybe even TikTok. Provided they have these platforms – and use their real name on them – you can uncover all sorts of details about who they are and what they're interested in. And depending on how much they share, and whether or not they use geotagging, you can find out more tangible details, too, such as where they live, which restaurants they frequent, and who their family members are. Think about what you'd have to do in order to find out this information without social media. You'd need to literally follow your crush around, listen to their conversations and possibly spend hours observing them from afar, all of which would legally be constituted as stalking. That is a criminal offence. Social media stalking is not.

The problem is that we have become so accustomed to being able to find out information about whoever we want whenever we want, that social media stalking doesn't even seem strange, despite the fact that it has normalised traits that are related to real-life stalking, such as violating a person's right to privacy. And while there is clearly a big difference between a bit of harmless Googling and committing a crime, it's important to recognise when a healthy curiosity about someone you are romantically interested in becomes unhealthy.

Social media stalking confession from my Twitter inbox #2
– Anonymous woman, late teens
I once met a guy on a night out who played for a premier league football team. I didn't remember his name but managed to source their team sheet and thus him. I didn't message him in the end, but it was nice to know where to find him if the impulse struck. Another time, I found a boy on Facebook who had been making eyes with me for months in the gym. I didn't know his name, where he was from, nothing. So I went on the gym's Instagram page and went through every follower – there were quite a few. It took some time, but eventually I found him, got in touch, and we went on a date. I wasn't even ashamed. I loved the feeling of getting to the end of my investigation.

Curiosity aside, I believe there's another reason why we are predisposed towards social media stalking when we fancy someone. Think about it. The most common way for people to meet today is by online dating, and when we use these apps and websites, we make choices about who we might want to meet based on profiles that come complete with a name, several photographs, and lots of random titbits of intel, such as their height, their religious beliefs and the fact they once ate an entire wheel of cheese. Whatever it may be, a person's online dating profile *always* comes armed with some kind of information about them. This leaves us with the impression that when we meet someone, we are entitled to know things about them without having to ask. So, when all we know is a person's name and hair colour, our instinct tells us to stalk them on social media to uncover more. Not just because we can (and we want to) but because we feel like we *must* if we're going to make a fair judgement on whether this is someone we should pursue romantically.*

Stalking someone you fancy on social media is very common. Sadly, there isn't a huge amount of research into the matter. But, anecdotally, I'll bet you or your friends have done it *at least* once. I've done it with every single person I've ever dated, though, Alex aside, I've always known their surname, so my social media stalking is less about detective work and more about being into someone and wanting to know more about them.

A 2017 survey of 1,000 people, conducted by Superdrug, found that 82 per cent of Europeans and 84 per cent of Americans have searched online for more information about someone they're attracted to, which, while a very small sample size, does support the theory that this is something a lot of people do. The survey also found that Facebook was the most used platform for social media stalking, which is unsurprising when you consider it has the most users of any platform (over

---

* A 2019 study published in the *Proceedings of the National Academy of Sciences* found that about 39 per cent of heterosexual couples reported meeting their partner online, compared to 22 per cent in 2009. Online dating was identified as the most common way that couples met one another. The study is based on a 2017 national survey of American adults.

two billion, in case you were wondering) and that people tend
to use their real names, unlike on Instagram or Twitter, where
they are more likely to come up with kitsch monikers, like
@oliviacooksorganic and @organicallyolivia (I went through
a phase of wanting to become a wellness influencer – it was
a short phase).*

In spite of all its faults, social media stalking does have its
perks, like giving you some potential talking points if conversation runs dry. Say you're on a first date with Alice, 27, from
Tinder. You're one hour in when you realise you've spent the
last twenty minutes discussing your respective commutes. Alice
gets the Victoria line but sometimes likes to mix it up by
doing some of her journey on the Northern line, but it's often
busier and noisier. You need to think of something fast in
order to stop this date becoming a dud. Suddenly, you
remember seeing a recent Instagram post from Alice of her at
an exhibition at the National Portrait Gallery. You went to
that exhibition last week. You bring it up, and just like magic,
you've gone from trading anecdotes on how long it takes to
get from Walthamstow to Brixton to comparing the portraiture
of Lucian Freud and Egon Schiele. Two hours later, you're
having amazing sex in Alice's kitchen because you couldn't
even wait to go upstairs.

When we spoke about social media stalking on the podcast,
Rachel raved about it. For her, it was the most efficient way
to vet the people she met on dating apps and satiate her
hunger for intel when she really liked someone. There was
one guy in particular who Rachel had been chatting to on
Hinge, where you can sometimes see someone's full name after

---

* Available at: https://onlinedoctor.superdrug.com/is-it-stalking/

they've matched with you, and after some extensive LinkedIn stalking, she learned that this guy was Head Boy at his school. That was a big tick. 'I thought it was a great sign because Head Boys are usually good eggs,' she said. 'They're overachievers, they're likeable, they have a lot of skills. And they're the type of person your parents would love. I just think that's who I'd want to be with.'

I asked Rachel what she would do if this guy brought up the fact that he'd been Head Boy on their date. Would she confess that she already knew? 'Of course not!' she replied as if it was absurd to even ask such a thing. That's the thing about social media stalking: it's supposed to be a secret. You can scroll through someone's profile until your fingers go numb, you're just not meant to tell them you're doing it. Otherwise, your date would go something like this.

Susie: So, what do you like to do on Sundays?

Charlie: Um, well, I guess the same kind of things most people like doing. Exercising, reading . . . there's this great place for brunch near my house that I think you'd love actually.

Susie: Oh yeah? Why's that?

Charlie: Well, because I noticed that in 2017 you posted on Instagram a lot about Black Dog in Manchester. And you often ordered the Vegan Full English. They have great vegan sausages at a place near my house. You went there actually in June for a bottomless brunch for one of your friends' birthdays. Her name was Kate Avery. She seems great, I really like the way she's decorated her living room. Ikea is really underrated.

Susie: Um.

Charlie: What's wrong?

Withholding how much you've stalked someone online before you meet them is integral to coming across as a normal human being. Because regardless of how harmless your intentions may be, as soon as you spell it out, social media stalking will make even the sanest of people sound sociopathic. The feeling of having someone regurgitate information about yourself to you is the closest thing that regular people have to empathising with celebrities, whose fans will purport to know everything about them, from what kind of dog they have to what type of non-dairy milk they like in their coffee. And celebrities do not date their fans. Bear that in mind the next time you consider telling your date you already know all about their friend's living room.

Social media stalking confession from my Twitter inbox #3
— Anonymous woman, early thirties
I once managed to find the husband of the woman my ex-boyfriend cheated on me with. I had his first name and used LinkedIn to find out where he worked. Once I found his company, I sent a message on the website's contact form asking for his e-mail. They gave it to me, and that's how I found out my boyfriend was cheating on me. It's safe to say we are no longer together.

That said, considering how common social media stalking is, it can be quite refreshing when someone owns up to it, so long as they go about it in the right way. I was talking to someone on Hinge recently and in his second message, he said that he'd been 'snooping' through my Instagram profile and started asking questions about my job. It was the first and only time someone has owned up to stalking me on social media, and there was something weirdly hot about it. Either that, or I just felt so flattered by the fact someone would 'snoop' through my Instagram feed that my ego was too fluffed up to care about anything else.

Depending on how much social media stalking you do, you can wind up making gross assumptions about a person's character. Take Instagram. Just because someone posts a beautiful photograph of a tree, it does not mean they are a photographer, that they love nature, or that they even care about the environment. They might just really like how that tree looks in that particular photo. Likewise, posting about the #MeToo movement or #BlackLivesMatter doesn't necessarily make someone an ally, it might just make them a virtue signaller. And posting a Story about a Lizzo gig doesn't mean you're a fan of Lizzo (if you're not, you're missing out). Maybe you just accompanied your best mate to the gig because they had a spare ticket, and you shared a photo from the night because the lighting looked cool. The thing is, unless the person you fancy is someone who writes lengthy captions about their personal life, pontificates about their politics, or regularly posts videos about their core values, you're never going to find out anything meaningful about them from their social media profile. It's a curated highlights reel, one that would be myopic to make any real judgements from.

Here are some of the assumptions we might make about potential partners based on their Instagram feeds.

> Post: A gym selfie taken in the changing rooms where the lighting is good. Half-clothed.
> Caption: 'Thank god it's Friday #FriYay #NoPainNoGain #GymThenGin'

Assumption: Narcissist who will shame you for eating beige food, even on weekends.

Post: Laughing in Clapham Common with an Aperol Spritz.
Caption: 'What rhymes with Aperol? #Weekend?'
Assumption: Wants to be an influencer and will convince you that taking photos of them is really fun.

Post: Smoking a roll-up cigarette made with a liquorice filter, beer in other hand. Eyes glazed over.
Caption: '#Vibes'
Assumption: Stoner who will abandon you to move to the Cayman Islands for three years to train as a reiki healer.

None of this really matters. At least not when you're looking for love. Sexual chemistry, intellectual compatibility, emotional connection . . . these are the things that are important. And you won't find them on someone's Instagram profile. But you will find out where they went for brunch on Saturday, what kind of exercise they do and what kind of wine they drink. The problem is that when you know so little about someone, it's very easy to form an opinion of their character based on such superficial information. And you know what they say about first impressions being hard to shake. By making such strong judgements about people based on their social media profiles, you could be missing out on all sorts of meaningful romantic connections. For example, you could really click with the stoner who dreams of being a reiki healer. You might even wind up in the Cayman Islands with them. But you'll never know if you don't give them a chance.

Of course, you can find out darker things about a person

by looking for information about them online. On the podcast, Rachel explained how she was going to meet a guy from Tinder but ended up cancelling because of something she saw about him on Google. 'I looked him up and found all these articles about [him] nearly having gone to prison for glassing someone in a club,' she said. We both acknowledged that there could be more to the story, and it's not entirely fair to judge someone you don't know based on one reported incident that you know no details about. But equally, would you want to go on a date with a stranger who once 'glassed someone in a club' when you could just as easily date one who hadn't?

It's not just potential partners who you might be inclined to stalk, either. For me, the people I'm most interested in stalking on social media are not the men I'm dating, but their ex-girlfriends. I'll go to the man's Instagram feed, work out who his exes are from obvious cues, like anniversary captions, happy birthday posts, or heart emojis, and proceed to spend the next five hours ruminating over how I am similar and different to these women – and crucially, what this means for my prospects with this man. I've since come to recognise this as a form of internalised misogyny – more on that in Chapter Six – but at the time, I thought I was just being insecure and nosy.

It doesn't help that I always seem to date people whose exes couldn't be more different from me. Ex-girlfriend highlights have included the dentist who became a very successful portrait artist and the Eva Green lookalike who dressed almost exclusively in Victorian clothing. And then there was the political commentator who had the words 'fucks like a pornstar' in her Twitter bio. I made harsh judgements on all these women based on their social media profiles, often creating stories in my head about what they must have done wrong in the relationship for it to come to an end. I took comfort in the fact that I seemed so different from them, considering their relationships had failed when mine was just beginning. But I never met any of these women. And if we dated the same men, we must have had more in common than I could glean from just their social media profiles.

Why is it that we've become so judgemental? Again, I think we can blame online dating, at least partly. Whether it's an app or a website, these platforms are full of users who you can jauntily swipe between faster than you can say 'aubergine emoji'. If a guy is less than six feet tall, forget it. Keep swiping until you find someone taller. If a woman has brown eyes but your dream woman has blue, why not keep looking until you find her? We have become very picky. So picky, in fact, that something as inane as height and eye colour can be the reason why you swipe right on one person and left on another. Nowadays, we're so conditioned to find our perfect 'match' that if someone doesn't meet our increasingly specific criteria we discard them. It should come as no surprise that we apply the same critical faculties to looking through a person's social media accounts, where, as on dating apps and websites, the most insignificant things can be an immediate turn-off.

The point of all this so far has been to explain why social media stalking can be detrimental when you want to fall in love. But it can be just as detrimental when you want to fall out of it. Look at break-ups. Processing the end of a relationship is wretched. Your friends will do everything in their power to help. They will drag you to parties to make small talk with strangers, order you another glass of wine when you're nearing your last sip. And they will gently nudge you towards 'getting under someone else' so you can let go of your ex. But that's a feat that is harder to achieve now than ever before. Thanks to social media, no one is ever really out of your life. Sure, you can block them. Maybe you can even delete all the photographs you posted of yourselves together, as discussed in the previous chapter. You could even close all your social media accounts. But none of this will curb the compulsion to see what an ex is up to in their post-you life. Do they seem happy? How's their career going? And crucially: have they moved on?

It's very common to stalk an ex on social media. So common, in fact, that Facebook has a tool designed to prevent users from doing so. There's even been some research into the issue. In 2015, Tara Marshall, a British psychologist at Brunel University, found that as many as one-third of people stalk an ex-partner on social media at least once a week.* 'Facebook surveillance is often perceived as a typical, harmless response to a break-up, but I've found that such Facebook stalking may obstruct the natural process of getting over an ex,' Marshall wrote at the time. Marshall's research proved that stalking an ex on social media will only make it that much harder to get over them. Since then, she has conducted follow-up research which suggests that people now use multiple platforms to obtain information about an ex-partner. I can attest to this,

---

* Tara Marshall, lecturer at Brunel University, *The Conversation*, December 2015.

given that, in the wake of my recent break-up, I blocked my ex from Instagram, so I would no longer have to see his Stories – a constant reminder of the pain I was trying to process. But I was kidding myself, because it was only a few days later that I realised we were still friends on Facebook and we still followed each other on Twitter, both of which provided ample information about what my ex was up to. I also realised that, should the compulsion strike me to check out my ex's Instagram feed, I could simply unblock him momentarily, and then block him again. He wouldn't even know – though he will now if he's reading this book.

There are different reasons as to why we want to stalk an ex on social media. Some people do it purely out of boredom or curiosity. These people, Marshall found, are less likely to do it frequently and are unlikely to experience any negative consequences as a result. However, those who do it more regularly are likely to do so out of jealousy, Marshall told me. 'They want to see if the ex-partner is involved with a new partner.' Some people, she added, are uncertain about the status of a former relationship – perhaps things feel unfinished – and so they will check their ex-partner's social media for clues. For me, it was a combination of curiosity and jealousy. I was curious about what my ex's life was like without me in it, and I was jealous of the people he could move on from me with.

This is unhealthy behaviour; that much is obvious. No one feels good when they realise they've wasted an hour stalking an ex's Instagram account, and another two sifting through that of the ex's new partner. It is the ultimate self-destructive act, one that Marshall's research suggests causes greater distress over the break-up, protracts longing for an ex and reignites sexual desire for them. And yet, it is somewhat addictive.

It doesn't help that you can actually see if your ex is also keeping an eye on you. On Instagram, for example, you can see everyone that has watched your Story. That includes exes, first loves, and maybe even people who have ghosted you – a practice that is known as 'orbiting'. There are also several paid-for apps that purport to tell you who has been looking at your Instagram profile. How on earth are you supposed to move on from someone when you can literally watch them watching you? The worst part is that you will inevitably draw meaning from their actions. I know I have, despite the fact that I sometimes watch Instagram Stories posted by people I haven't spoken to in ten years and so should know better. But for some reason, if I see that an ex is watching my Instagram Story, I take it as a sign that they still harbour feelings towards me. Take Jack, for example. It took me years to get over that almost-relationship. And one of the reasons for this was that I kept finding ways to tell myself that he *must* still be interested in me. The fact that he always watched my Instagram Story was one of them.

Surveying an ex's social media platforms is a bad habit we all need to kick. But it's not as simple as unfollowing or removing your ex as a friend (you can still view their profile), deleting the apps off your phone (you can still access them via a web browser), or even blocking your ex from all your social media accounts (you'll still be able to see their profile if you log out and search for them on Google). Some people even create fake social media accounts to keep an eye on their ex's channels without them knowing – a recent survey conducted by a US cybersecurity firm found that out of 2,000 people, almost half confessed to having alternative accounts purely to cyberstalk ex or current partners.*

The key is to ask yourself 'why'. What is compelling you to cyberstalk your ex? Is it just that you're nosy? Or is it that you're in denial about not being over them? If this is the case, the real question you need to ask yourself is not 'how can I stop stalking my ex on social media', it's 'how can I move on from my break-up'? It's a complex question with even more complex answers. Someone once told me that it takes half the time you were with a partner to get over them – but that means that if you're coming out of, say, a four-year relationship, it will take two years to move on. I refuse to subscribe to this myth, not least because I've been known to spend months (and sometimes years) mourning relationships that lasted for just a few weeks or ones that existed almost entirely in my head.

When I interviewed the American psychologist Guy Winch, author of *How to Fix a Broken Heart*, for the *Independent*, he shared some valuable science-backed tips for getting over someone. He explained how studies of MRI scans of the brain have found that going through a break-up, or 'withdrawing from romantic love', as he put it, can activate the same mechanisms in the brain that are activated when an addict is going through withdrawal from drugs and alcohol. That's why it feels so torrid when you're trying to move on from someone you're still in love with – you literally have to wean yourself off them as though they were an addictive substance.

* NortonLifeLock survey, 2020, 2,000 Americans surveyed. Available at: https://investor.nortonlifelock.com/About/Investors/press-releases/press-release-details/2020/Nearly-Half-of-Americans-Admit-to-Stalking-an-Ex-or-Current-Partner-Online/default.aspx

Among Winch's list of tips for getting over someone – the first of which was to not check their social media – he advised avoiding inventing explanations about why the break-up happened. 'Accept any explanation that fits the facts and keeps your self-esteem intact, such as they were unwilling to commit, they allowed themselves to drift emotionally and didn't bring up what was happening until it was too late, or they were just not the person you thought they were,' he said. Winch also suggested reaching out to friends for support and removing any reminders of the relationship that might cause you further pain, such as texts and photos. One of the things I have always done in the wake of a break-up is to delete all the texts and WhatsApp messages between myself and an ex. Otherwise I wind up scrolling through them and re-reading them all, tracing our relationship right from its infancy to its dissolution, and trying to work out what went wrong. It helps to delete their number, too, something I learned with my most recent ex after I found myself frequently clicking on his name in my WhatsApp just to see if he was 'online', because if he was, I would just stare at that word as if it made me close to him again.

When we spoke about how to get over a break-up on the podcast, Olympic athlete Victoria Pendleton said that she finds it helpful to physically challenge herself. So, while she was in the process of splitting up from her husband of five years, Scott Gardner, Pendleton went to climb Mount Everest. 'The divorce had been going through processing for years [before she announced it publicly when she returned from Everest] but I'd just been keeping it on the quiet really because I didn't really need any additional pressure and stress with all the Everest preparations,' she said. During the climb, Pendleton suffered from hypoxia, which is when the brain is deprived of oxygen. As a result, she could not complete the climb. A knock-on effect from hypoxia is depression, which Pendleton also suffered on her return to the UK. 'That was twinned with the fact that I thought I had everything to do with my divorce in a box and sorted. I was like, "yep, I've got this". And then I came back to reality quite literally and it shook me up a lot. It was a very difficult time of uncertainty and for me the idea of putting myself in a different environment was something I felt I really needed to do.'

Pendleton packed up and went on another adventure to Costa Rica for an all-female fitness retreat for six weeks. Her close friend Sophie Everard, who runs the Mad to Live retreat that Pendleton went on, explained that a lot of the women who come on her retreats are going through a break-up. 'My ops manager and I actually say to each other, "if we had a pound for every time we had a lady come on our retreats who's going through a break-up, or considering it, we'd be millionaires",' Everard said on the podcast. 'They're seeking solace in some kind of way.' There's something about doing extreme sports that builds resilience, which is very necessary when it comes to overcoming a break-up. Take surfing, which is one of the key activities that Everard teaches on her retreats. 'You're constantly being knocked down by waves, falling off things, maybe taking tumbles, but you get up again, you get up again, you get up again. And that's sort of teaching you that you do have the resilience to pick yourself up and keep going.'

When you're trying to process a break-up, it can be very tempting to focus all your energy on what you did wrong, Pendleton added. 'It's very easy to lay the blame on you.

"There's something wrong with me, why don't they love me, why don't they want me." And that doesn't just disappear. Everyone's like: just be patient. I am horribly impatient.'

Extreme sports might have helped Pendleton deal with a break-up, but the thing that helps you could be completely different. Maybe you'll dedicate yourself to a work project or pick up a new creative hobby. For me, the trick to getting over my most recent break-up has been running, meditating and putting all my energy into work and friendships. It's not a fast process – healing never is – but these things do help. What most certainly does not help is scrolling through my ex's Instagram feed at 2 a.m. trying to work out if he's shagging any of the people he's just started following.

Chapter Five
Love at First Swipe

It took three months for me to realise something was off with Will. We had met on Bumble. I made a joke about a dorky photo of him ziplining; he said I had a nice smile. Soon we were talking about our favourite music festivals, why *In Rainbows* is the most underrated Radiohead album, and which breed of dog we'd rather be – and why this was not necessarily the same as the breed you'd own. He asked for my number, and we moved to WhatsApp.

This was my first foray into dating apps and so far, it seemed fairly straightforward. Will was a polite feminist with green eyes. We seemed to have quite a bit in common, which was enough for me to ask him to meet for a drink. 'Can you do Tuesday or Wednesday?' he replied. I was working late on Wednesday, so suggested we meet at a pub in Soho at 8.30 p.m. 'That's a bit late for midweek. Can we do another day?' 'Of course! Let's reschedule,' I wrote back, wondering what kind of 25-year-old thinks 8.30 p.m. is too late for midweek. Six days later, we still hadn't set a date. I tried again: 'Right, Thursday?' He was busy. 'Wednesday?' Not sure, he could let me know on the day. 'No worries.'

This painful back and forth persisted for weeks. Whenever Will was free, I was busy. And vice versa. Soon, the flirting had fizzled, and all we spoke about was each other's schedules. *Is this what marriage feels like?* Finally, he suggested a date I could do. We planned to meet in a cosy north London pub. Three hours before we were meant to see each other (at the very reasonable hour of 7 p.m.) he texted me: 'I'm so sorry, I thought I'd be fine by this evening, but I've got a case of the man flu. Can we rearrange? I swear I never do this.'

Will ghosted me shortly after that. My last message to him was a question about his weekend plans. Two weeks later, he hadn't even read it. I know what you're supposed to do in this scenario. You're supposed to go all sassy girl emoji: roll your eyes, flick your hair, buy a new dress and then meet a random person named Jude in a pub, call him Rory, and snog his face off. But I'd never been properly ghosted before, and I was not willing to accept defeat. I did the one thing your friends will always tell you not to do in this situation: I messaged him. 'Did you die?'

He replied the next day. 'Sorry I've been so shit. I don't want to waste any more of your time. I'm recently out of a relationship and don't want to lead you on any further. You seem far too lovely for rubbish treatment from me as I'm not looking for something serious (not that you necessarily are!) so I think it's best we don't go for a drink. Hope that makes vague sense and we're cool.'

'Oh my god that is SO understandable,' I replied. 'Poor you, hope you're alright, mate. Funnily enough, I'm in a similar situation. Lol. See ya.' I was not in a similar situation because I hadn't had sex in two years. I swore off dating apps for life and then downloaded Hinge the following week.

Roughly one in three people have used either dating apps or websites – this figure increases to almost half among 18-to

29-year-olds.* More than 340 million people have downloaded Tinder since its launch. You can find 476 million on Badoo. A further 95 million on Bumble. And 70 million on happn. You'll find seven million people on Plenty of Fish, six million on Grindr, and four million on Her.† Almost all these platforms work in a similar way. One profile appears, usually with a photograph, a first name and some random bits of information, like how often they drink, whether they take drugs, what their religious beliefs are, their political leanings and sometimes even how frequently they work out and what star sign they are. You make a judgement on whether this is someone you're likely to vibe with, and swipe either right (for yes) or left (for no). Then another profile pops up. And then another. And then another. Welcome to the new sexual marketplace, where love and sex are traded as easily as stocks and bonds.

It seems so easy, doesn't it? If not to find someone to fall in love with, then at least to find someone to shag. And yet, as I mentioned earlier, millennials apparently have less sex than previous generations. In 2018, an article on this subject titled 'the sex recession' on *The Atlantic* went viral.‡ It outlined research which suggested that young people today have fewer sexual partners than those in Generation X had at a similar age. There were a lot of possible reasons why, from surging anxiety rates and the hook-up culture, to violent pornography and environmental oestrogens leaked by plastics. One reason

---

* Pew Research Center, 2020. Survey of 4,860 US adults conducted in October 2019. The research found that the number of people who have used dating apps and websites in the US has risen over time.
† These figures were as of June 2020.
‡ Kate Julian, 'Why are young people having so little sex?', *The Atlantic*, December 2018.

given was dating apps. The piece pointed to research from Tinder, which stated that the company logs 1.6 billion swipes a day, but just 26 million matches. The implication was that while a lot of people were swiping, only a few were actually talking to people, let alone meeting up with them. What was going wrong?

No dating app is the same. There are the major players, some of which I mentioned earlier, and while many of them are fairly interchangeable, a few stand out. Like happn, which shows you single people you've recently crossed paths with. And Hinge, where you have to fill your profile with answers to prompts that can be anything from 'I'm looking for . . .' and 'I take pride in . . .', to 'A shower thought I recently had was . . .' and 'I'm the type of texter who . . .'. And then there's Bumble, where, in heterosexual pairings, the woman has to initiate the conversation. This USP relies on the archaic idea that men only ever make the first move. Obviously, they don't. But this shtick was enough to convince me that Bumble was the app where all the hot feminist men hung out – so that was the first one I ever downloaded. Some apps purport to facilitate relationships (Hinge's tagline is 'designed to be deleted') while others market themselves as hook-up apps. Take OKCupid's 2018 marketing campaign, which used the slogan 'DTF', an acronym commonly translated to 'down to fuck', but which here was replaced with phrases like: 'Down to Fall Head Over Heels' and 'Down to Furiously Make Out'. Meanwhile, some of Tinder's recent ads have carried slogans including: 'Congrats on your big break-up', 'Single does what Single wants' and 'Single never has to go home early'.

There are a lot of niche apps, too, to suit every sexual predilection and prejudice. If you like men with beards, for example, you can download Bristlr. If you're into firefighters, nurses, police officers, or anyone who works in uniform, try Uniform Dating. And if you have sex dreams about bacon and bacon dreams about sex, look no further than Sizzl, an app that connects you with like-minded bacon lovers and asks you to state how you like your bacon cooked on your profile. There are also apps that you have to apply to get onto. Like Toffee Dating, for those who went to private school, and Luxy, which recruits 'high-end singles'. Then there's Raya, the Soho House of dating apps that attracts actors, models, musicians and, well, people who look like actors, models, and musicians. Cara Delevingne, Zach Braff and Amy Schumer are all rumoured to have been members.

Segregating single people according to their class, education and interests is not only creepy and dystopian, it's also counterproductive to helping people find love. This is because very often, the people we fall in love with take us completely by surprise. They are not the ones we'd look for, but the ones we might miss. Ask any couple who met offline what they thought of one another when they met, and I'll guarantee you at least half will say they never expected to end up together. They'll say things like: 'I never thought I'd date a banker', 'I didn't think I could possibly like someone who lived outside of London', and 'I never suspected I'd fall in love with someone who eats tofu for fun'.

Unexpected pairings work; sometimes they're the best ones. But dating apps render them impossible, because they rely on your ability to predict the kind of person you should be with. And those predictions are often based on superficial factors, such as what a person looks like, whether or not they went to Oxbridge and how frequently they eat bacon. They also encourage you to make fast decisions – *very* fast. Think about how quickly you swipe through people's profiles when you're using a dating app. Say you give each profile two seconds of consideration time – I usually only take one second, but let's be generous here. If you spend ten minutes on an app, you'll get through 1,200 profiles in a single sitting. That's enough people to fill twenty-one London buses.

Some people will say that you can identify whether you're attracted to someone in as little as one-fifth of a second. Attraction, they say, is instant. And while there are studies to back this up, they are all based on real-life interactions as opposed to those between people separated by screens.* But attraction is not always immediate. How could it be? When we all know those couples who fell in love after five years of friendship? Or those who couldn't stand each other at first? In real life, it can take minutes, months and maybe even years to decide whether you fancy someone. On a dating app, we make these decisions in a few seconds.† And when you make decisions quickly, particularly so many of them at once, you're bound to make mistakes.

Let's take a look at dating app profiles. This is something we've spoken about on the podcast quite a bit. When Rachel hosted the show with me, we used to have a regular segment called

---

* Neuroimaging of Love: fMRI Meta-Analysis Evidence toward New Perspectives in Sexual Medicine, 2010. Available at: https://onlineli-brary.wiley.com/doi/abs/10.1111/j.1743-6109.2010.01999.x
† Martin Graff and Emily Welsby, 'Decision Making in Tinder', University of South Wales, 2019. This study found that men and women take an average of 1.4 seconds to make a decision on Tinder about whether to swipe left or right on someone.

'bio of the week', in which we would read out our favourite bios that we'd seen on people's dating app profiles, either chosen by us or sent in by a listener. That segment feels outdated now, given that a lot of dating apps allow users to divulge so much more about themselves as opposed to just their age, height and a short 'bio'. But at the time, the apps most frequently used by us and our listeners were Tinder, Bumble and Grindr, all of which were bio-only at the time.

Here were some of my favourite bios of the week as sent in by our lovely listeners:

10 points if you can guess my name

You know who else likes food and travel? Everyone

Once apologised to an automatic door

And here were some of the worst:

Saving lives and shagging nines

I'm really picky, so don't get offended

That's my niece in the photo

People write a lot of weird stuff on their dating app profiles. One of my favourite places to gawp at some of the more ridiculous creations is on an Instagram account called @Tories_of_Bumble. It is, as the name suggests, a place littered with profiles from Bumble, Hinge and more that clearly indicate that the user is either a Tory or a massive dickhead, or both. Think investment bankers in top hats sharing photos from what one can only assume was a straightforward shooting weekend.

Here's a selection of bios featured on the account:

Equally comfortable at a Brixton gig as a country black tie dinner

Investment banker with a net worth of over £3.5bn. Interested now?

Conservative in the booth, liberal in the sheets

On Saturday at 2am you can find me getting absolutely chateauxed on the good stuff

A social cause I care about: The wellbeing of the top 0.1%

It's easy to poke fun, but what you choose to write on your dating app profile is important. Because it's the one thing you can offer other than your photos. Whatever you choose to say will inevitably say a lot about you and could be the very thing that leads someone to swipe either right or left.

When Louise Troen – Bumble's then-Head of Communications – came on the podcast, she offered Rachel and me some advice on our own dating app profiles. Rachel's profile got a five-star review. She had nailed her profile photo – a well-lit shot of her wearing red lipstick with her hand on her hips. The other photos showed her doing various activities, like diving and skiing and eating brunch. These photos reflected Rachel's interests, which is exactly what a dating app profile should do. As for her bio, she had written: 'Peanut butter aficionado, speaker of French and

German, optimist, coriander averse, 5'9"'. This was accompanied by a series of emojis: a clinking champagne flute, an avocado and a woman weightlifting. Troen thought it was great. My profile received a different review. My main photo was of me wearing a helmet, so you could hardly see my face. That was my first mistake. The second was a photo where I was dressed as a mad hatter – costumes are bad, too – and the third was a snap of me sunken into an inflatable sofa at Glastonbury Festival. I realised that in all my photos, I'd subconsciously tried to conceal what I looked like. This was, Troen told me, rather unhelpful considering other single users would need to see what I looked like in order to make a fair judgement of me. My bio was bad too: 'Be nice, I'll probably write about you'. I was right, of course, given that I've now written a book containing stories about almost everyone I've ever dated. But I was told that such a statement might come across as intimidating. I changed it to 'be nice' instead and was very annoyed when people still weren't.

Even though Troen insisted that Rachel's profile was a perfect example of how a dating app profile should look, it still did her a disservice. At least it did in my view. I know Rachel very well. If I saw her dating app profile without having ever met her, I would think she was a bit, shall we say, generic. That might just mean she's not the woman for me, which is fine. But I also happen to know that the first time I met Rachel, there was absolutely nothing generic about her. Her energy was infectious. She was interesting, intelligent and even though she spoke at 100 miles per hour and barely came up for breath, we were in fits of giggles within minutes, as if we'd known each other for years. I'm aware that Rachel and I were not on a date when we met, but my point is this: we can obtain so much more information from someone when they are physically in front of us. How they sound when they talk. How their face moves. How they smell. How it feels when we exchange eye contact with them or laugh with them. In short, we get a much more rounded view of who they are, and whether they are compatible with us. On an app, we get none of this. The first impression you get from a person's dating app profile is always going to be substantially different, and less accurate, compared to a first impression that you'd get in-person.

Dating confession from my Bumble inbox #1:

[Context: he had a photo of himself eating a rainbow bagel in his profile and his occupation was 'filmmaker'.]

Me: Do rainbow bagels really taste like a rainbow?

Christopher: They really don't. They just taste like regular bagels.

Me: That's a shame. They've missed a trick there. Almost like they've made them just for the 'gram.

Christopher: I think the baking community of Brick Lane is heavy on the 'gram. I just haven't found their profiles yet.

Me: They definitely are. What kind of films do you make?

[One month later]

Me: Short films then? That's cool. I hear they're making a comeback.

Christopher: Really sorry! Don't have notifications on this app. What's your number?

Me: I was expecting a laugh at my excellent joke but no bother. [This is the bit where I put my phone number]. You can distribute your laughs via text/WhatsApp.

[One month later – still no text from Christopher]

Me: I smell catfish.

A dating app profile is a curated, cherry-picked version of a person. It doesn't matter how much information you pile on there. By its very definition, it can only ever be a superficial representation of who you are, because you choose the photos you share and the information you divulge. This was one of the reasons why author Bolu Babalola swore off dating apps altogether, as she told me when she came on the podcast to discuss her book *Love in Colour*. 'I tried them and I actually feel sick whenever I use them,' she said, recalling how she would sit down to write her bio and feel like it didn't reflect who she actually was. 'It's just not me. There was so much freedom when I realised, "oh that's just not compatible with who I am". Because at first I felt like a weirdo because everyone's using them. But just because it works for other people doesn't mean it works for you.'

When the author Raven Smith joined me on the podcast to discuss dating apps, he described them like a game. 'You're trying to win,' he said. 'And [if things don't work out], you just have another life. It's not that real because it's just this flat screen. In the same way you die online, you just come back to life and date again.' It really does feel like you're playing a game when you're on a dating app, swiping from one person to the next. Maybe that's why we tend to use them so mindlessly. We swipe on the loo, at work and while we're watching TV. It's almost always a secondary activity and rarely ever a primary one. Which is why, when we're busy swiping through hundreds of dating app profiles every few minutes, it's actually rather difficult to see these people as human beings. Instead, they become interchangeable ciphers in this strange game we're all playing.

*   *   *

The overwhelming amount of choice on dating apps can be paralysing and creates what the American psychologist Barry Schwartz would call the paradox of choice. As he puts it in his 2004 book, *The Paradox of Choice – Why More is Less*, with regards to online dating, 'a large array of options may diminish the attractiveness of what people *actually* choose, the reason being that thinking about the attractions of some of the unchosen options detracts from the pleasure derived from the chosen one.' In other words, having so many single users at our disposal makes it almost impossible to pick just one of them, making monogamy very difficult indeed. Casual sex, on the other hand, is much easier, making it unsurprising that researchers say the rise of online dating has led to an overall decrease in commitment.*

This extensive amount of choice has another, more insidious, drawback, because it changes the way we treat one another. Research has found that seeing so many users at once when we're on a dating app fosters a culture of disposability. It's a bit like fast fashion.† Swipe right on one person (buy a £4 top from boohoo), see if there's a vibe (does it look nice on?), if you're not feeling it (it doesn't look nice on), ghost them (throw the boohoo top away), and start swiping again (go on Missguided). All of this means we're less likely to settle for anyone, or any £4 top. 'We are constantly told that something better is around the corner,' said Smith, who met his husband IRL before the dating app boom. 'I think

---

* Dan Slater, *Love in the Time of Algorithms*, 2013.
† In 2011, Mark Brooks, consultant to online dating companies, published the results of an industry survey titled 'How Has Internet Dating Changed Society?' and concluded that 'internet dating has made people more disposable'.

about my grandma and buying a red jumper. There's two shops on her high street in the Isle of Wight. So, you either get the red jumper from Woolies, which is a bit too long, or you get the red jumper from the knitting shop which is just a bit too red. And you just choose between the two of them. In this culture, we are constantly scrolling for the perfect red jumper. We just won't stop until our perfection is catered to.'

The consequences of this are clear to see. Whether it's clothes or people, when we view something as disposable, we're more likely to treat it, and them, poorly. Think about all of those horrible so-called dating 'trends'. In addition to those I've already mentioned (ghosting, orbiting and breadcrumbing), there's stashing (when someone you're dating doesn't want you to meet their family), cookie-jarring (maintaining several backup options in case your current relationship doesn't work out) and curving (this is like ghosting but instead of disappearing forever, the person you're dating will gradually phase you out). The behaviours that these terms describe are almost always callous and cruel, and they have arisen as a direct consequence of dating app culture, because dating apps are often the ones making them up. Every few months, I receive a press release from one of the major apps or websites listing at least ten new trends to note. They can be based on anything, and I mean *anything*. There are those based on popular culture characters (Elsa'd – when someone slowly stops replying to your texts and eventually freezes you out) and there are those based on the time of year (Marleying – getting in touch with an ex just because you don't want to be alone at Christmas).

I've been the victim of these 'trends', but I've also been the perpetrator. There was the time I was on a desperately dull Bumble date with a man who was not as funny in person as he was on WhatsApp. So, I went to the loo and asked my friend to call in five minutes with an 'emergency' – a classic date escape that is as transparent as it is uncreative. Then, when he messaged me later that night, I ghosted him. There was also the time I asked an ex to meet up purely to see if it would offer clarity on a fledgling relationship with someone I'd just met on Hinge – I don't think there's a word for this, but there should be because it's not nice. I wouldn't behave this way with people I met in real life, but something about having met them via a dating app made me feel like I could do whatever I wanted without consequences.

> **Dating confession from my Bumble inbox #2:**
> [Context: he had 'good at lovemaking' as his occupation.]
> Me: Good at Lovemaking . . . come off it. Surely not a job.
> Simon: It's an honest existence. I don't question your occupations.
> Me: Journalism isn't an honest occupation. Fake news etc.
> Simon: Yes, but you sound like a hack with a difference.
> Me: You can literally taste the difference.
> Simon: Can I lick your LinkedIn profile?

Even once you're on a date with someone you met on an app, it feels less exciting than when you're on a date with someone you met sporadically. Apps completely strip the dating experience of any spontaneity, as everyone is on them for the same reason: to meet someone. There's no confusion about that. Not only can this make the actual dates themselves feel a little forced, but it can also create pressure, as Babalola said on the podcast. 'There's this [feeling] of "oh we're both here to meet somebody and we're both hoping that we click".'

None of this is incidental. In fact, this is exactly how dating apps want us to behave, think and feel when we use them. Hence why they send journalists like me the aforementioned press releases, so they can be used to write articles with headlines such as '10 NEW MILLENNIAL DATING TRENDS YOU NEED TO KNOW NOW'. These lists remind people of the authority that dating apps have over the way we date now. The fact that all these trends have strange and playful names simply adds to this idea that modern dating is a game, one that apps really don't want you to win.

The less success we have on dating apps, the more successful dating apps become. If we were all to magically fall in love on Tinder, Tinder would no longer need to exist. It's no wonder, then, why the dating app experience is so bloody difficult. It's *supposed* to be that way. They aren't selling us actual romance, rather the idea of it. And what could be more seductive than that? So yes, we're supposed to be super picky so that we never find someone that's good enough. We're supposed to go on terrible dates so we'll look harder for good ones. And we're supposed to become addicted to swiping so that we'll never stop.

In Florence Given's book, *Women Don't Owe You Pretty*, she likens ghosting to capitalism. 'Capitalism is a system which almost exactly and entirely replicates narcissistic abuse,' she explained when she came on the podcast. 'It instils fear in people and creates insecurities and then profits from those insecurities.' That is how ghosting works. 'Not always, but when it is done in a way that someone will avoid you and then come back and then avoid you and come back (this is sometimes called 'haunting'), that's why I said it's like capitalism. Because they almost plant this insecurity inside of you that you've done something wrong by not talking to you for a couple of weeks. There's this passive aggressive silent treatment and you internalise all of that. It's happened to me, I've been ghosted a few times and it makes you feel shit. Only this person can heal this insecurity in you because they have the supply, only they give you what you need to feel secure again.'

Dating confession from my Bumble inbox #3:

[Context: He said that cigarette emojis were 'basic' in his bio and his profile photo was of himself wearing a flower crown.]

Me: What makes cigarette emojis basic, then?

Billy: I think it's the element of danger

Me: Same for the flower crown?

Billy: If you're suffering from hayfever, then yes!

Me: Which festival warranted the excuse to wear that thing?

Billy: I was in the park with mates and took the photo as a bit of a Tinder piss take. That's why my T-shirt sleeve is rolled up, too.

Me: I hate to be the person to break this to you. But this is actually Bumble.

If ghosting is like capitalism, where does that leave dating apps? Think about it. These apps make money by promising love to single people. They provide the marketplace in which they can do this under the guise that this marketplace is completely transparent – here are all the single people in the world, now go and copulate freely and happily – but it isn't. There are so many hurdles that render it opaque. Due to this, people find themselves returning to the apps again and again.

In economic terms, dating apps present users with an unlimited supply and then do their best to make sure that demand doesn't peter out. It's textbook capitalism masked as a potentially great love story.

We had a segment on the show called 'dating disaster', where we would read out some of the terrible – but hilarious – dating stories listeners had sent us. It felt appropriate to reignite it for the book. So, without further ado, here are some of the best dating disasters I've been sent in the process of writing this book. And yes, all of them met their dates on dating apps.

A few years ago, I got a message on Scruff from a guy who just said 'Sorry for the late reply, I've been stupidly busy at work.' I looked at the timestamps of our conversation. My original message to him had been sent two years prior to his reply. I love that he just passed it off as if two years is a normal time to respond to something or didn't even pretend to start a new conversation. Where was he working, an oil rig? Anyway, I was at a party one New Year's Eve and we were all sharing our stories of hook-up app disasters. I got my phone out and told my friends this story, showed them the screenshots, we all had a big laugh about it. A little while later I got chatting to one of the guys at the party, whom I hadn't met before, and he just meekly raised his hand and said 'yeah . . . that was me'. – Male, 24

I went on a date about three years ago with a guy called Jack. He had told me a few things about himself to note: he was 30, he lived alone in London, he played rugby, he liked music, he was 5ft9. When we met, he looked nothing like his photos and was shorter than me. Now, I am not shallow but this wasn't what I was expecting and so I was a bit thrown. But I thought, do you know what, it'll be a good date regardless. I was so wrong. We got through the basics fairly quickly, and it came to light that he didn't live on his own, or in London, but in fact he lived with his parents, somewhere over an hour away. Again, nothing wrong with living with your parents, but his reasons were: he plays rugby two to three times during the week and doesn't get home until about 8.30 p.m. So on those days, his mum cooks him dinner. When he asked if I wanted to get some food, or another drink, I said no. He got up to go to the toilet, came back with two drinks and said, 'I was hungry so I've ordered some food.' What did he order? A fucking roast dinner. I sat and watched him eat his roast before making an excuse to leave. He insisted on walking to the station with me (I actually was near enough my flat to walk home but decided to divert to a station). I endured a fifteen minute walk with him and to my horror, he said he was getting on the train too. I rambled about suddenly deciding to walk and then he went in for a kiss. I swerved. He texted to say he thought it had gone well and we should do it again. — Female, 28

At the beginning of the year, I matched with a girl on Tinder and we went on a few good dates. On our fourth date, I went to hers and she cooked me dinner. The food — vegan pasta bake — was delicious and it was going well. We went to her room and had sex, but a few things were off. There were dick-shaped candles on her bedside table, empty condom wrappers on the floor, and pieces of pita *bread in her bed. She also told me that I taste like Ribena. I left feeling a bit strange. A few days passed and she ghosted me. I was slightly confused, so my friend lent me her phone and we looked at her Instagram account, which she'd blocked me from seeing, and it turns out she had a boyfriend. The weirdest part is still the Ribena comment. She said it was a good thing because she never drinks Ribena and can't afford to buy branded squash, but I still find it strange. – Female, 19*

I was talking to a guy I met on an app for a month or so and when we finally met up, he was two hours late. I would have cancelled at this point, but he was coming to the bar at the bottom of my street and I had nothing better to do. He arrived absolutely hammered. The entire date, all he did was talk about himself. And then went on a rant about how he would never find anyone worthwhile from a dating app because it was 'embarrassing'. I pointed out that we were on a dating app date . . . he said this was 'different'. We stayed at the bar till closing and he conveniently realised he couldn't get home from my area that late at night, unless he got on a two-hour bus. I made him order an Uber and while he was waiting for it, he said he was going to shit himself. I was so desperate to get rid of him at this point, so I let him shit in my house. – Female, 25

Everyone has one of these stories or knows someone who does. I received so many more that could not be squeezed into the pages of this book. Like the woman whose Tinder date peed himself on the night bus while sitting next to her. The man who responded to 'been to any good gigs?' with 'I just saw a dead body' after they'd just met. The woman whose Hinge date had green teeth, something he had not disclosed in his profile. The man who had a nosebleed all over the menu in a Michelin star restaurant. The woman who accidentally booty-called two men on the same night only to open the door and find them chatting about football. For some people, dating apps have become so gamified that it can be difficult to take the dates themselves seriously, particularly when you wind up with stories like these.

Of course, not all the stories I received were funny. Some were very dark. That's the thing about dating apps. Like all online platforms, they are a space in which vile behaviour thrives. I don't just mean ghosting, orbiting and so on – those things tend to happen as a result of dating app culture, and not necessarily on dating apps themselves. I mean the instances when you're still speaking to someone you've never actually met. Someone you feel a physical distance from. Someone with whom you can still maintain relative anonymity. This is an environment in which your actions feel inconsequential. You can say anything you like, be anyone you want to be, and nobody you know will ever have to know about it.

The term 'catfishing' takes its name from a 2010 documentary, *Catfish*, about a man named Yaniv (Nev) Schulman, who developed an online relationship with an attractive 19-year-old woman named Megan, only to later discover that no such woman existed. The person he had been talking to was actually a 39-year-old woman named Angela, who had an estranged daughter named Megan, but had pretended to be a fictionalised version of her in order to establish a relationship with Nev. That's catfishing.

While the circumstances surrounding catfishing can

sometimes be illegal, catfishing alone – using a fake social media profile to start an online romance – is not recognised as a criminal offence in the UK.* And so it often happens under the radar. There have been several high profile victims of catfishing in recent years, all of varying degrees of severity and with different outcomes. They include the singer Casey Donovan, who had a six-year telephone relationship with someone pretending to be the NBA star Chris Andersen – her catfish wound up serving twelve months in prison for imper-sonation and extortion. Then there was Carly Ryan, the 15-year-old Australian schoolgirl who was murdered by a serial paedophile that befriended her on MySpace under a false identity. And then there are the many cases that we don't read about in newspapers, ones that don't necessarily result in criminal charges or brutal murders but can still create long-lasting psychological damage for the victim.

On the podcast, I interviewed a woman who had been catfished. Karina had been with her boyfriend for four months when she realised he was not who she thought he was. In an article written for the *Independent* about her experience, she referred to him as Sam. The couple were living together when Karina stumbled upon Sam's passport, only to find that he had lied about his age. 'That was the first red flag,' she told me. The second was a corker. Karina was using Sam's iPad when she noticed a website for obtaining 'burner numbers', i.e. fake phone numbers that people use to sign up to various services, thus enabling them to maintain complete anonymity online. Karina

---

* A petition launched by a victim of catfishing, Anna Rowe, is calling for it to become a recognised crime under the Fraud Act, Communications Act and Sex Offences Act. It has over 52,000 signatures as of March 2021.

spotted one that was attached to a Hinge account, and used it to log into the app. The account was linked to a profile under the name of Alex, a completely different person to Sam. Different age, different photos, different job. It soon transpired that 'Alex' was just one of Sam's many fake identities that he used to speak to women on several dating apps, sometimes even talking to the same women using different accounts to see which identity they were most attracted to. 'I didn't see it coming at all,' Karina said. 'He was very good at what he did and making you think that he was head over heels for you.' What she found most frustrating was that after confronting Sam, he was unable to explain himself. 'I can't rationalise his behaviour, I've tried,' Karina told me. 'I've spoken to him at length about what he did, but he was never able to give me a direct answer. We kind of reached a conclusion together where I just begged him to get help because I thought he needed to speak to a professional.'

There's not a huge amount of research into catfishing, particularly when it is of a social nature – deception in the absence of financial fraud – like Karina's and Nev's experiences. One survey from 2016 found that more than half of online dating users have come across a fake profile, which would suggest that social catfishing is fairly common.* One Australian study conducted in 2018 looked into the motivations behind catfishing behaviour.† Out of twenty-seven people who self-identified as a catfish, 41 per cent said loneliness was their main incentive. Others cited self-esteem issues. 'I actually consider myself ugly

---

* Which? survey of 1,000 people, 2016. Available at: https://www. which.co.uk/news/2016/02/fake-and-suspicious-profiles-rife-on-dating-sites-432850/
† Eric Vanman of the University of Queensland writing in *The Conversation*, July 2018.

and unattractive,' one participant said, who added: 'The only way I have had relationships has been online and with a false identity.' Another concurred: 'If I try to send my real, unedited pictures to anyone that seems nice, they stop responding to me. It's a form of escapism, or a way of testing what life would be like if you were the same person but more physically attractive.' Some people wanted to fake not just their identity but also their gender in order to explore alternative identities and sexualities. And some simply wanted to escape.

While I don't want to paint a sympathetic picture of catfish, it's interesting to note from the research that these people seem to have all faced some sort of discrimination. That is what they feel vindicates their abhorrent and manipulative behaviour. We know that dating apps perpetuate a looks-first approach to romance. So, for people who feel insecure about the way they look or are worried about judgement and prejudice based on their looks, they may think that one way out is to just be someone else entirely.

Racism thrives on dating apps. It can manifest in numerous ways, from racist messages and fetishisation to colourism and bios ruling out a particular ethnicity. There's been quite a lot of research done in the area, with much highlighting the prevalence of racism among the LGBT+ dating app community in particular. Take Grindr, for example, where 96 per cent of users have seen at least one profile featuring some kind of racial discrimination, while more than half said they themselves had been victims of racism on the app.*

---

* 2015 article. Available at: https://link.springer.com/article/10.1007/s10508-015-0487-3

It certainly didn't help that until June 2020, the app had an ethnicity filter, which meant people could literally specify that they wanted to date people of certain races, and not date people of others. 'It seems like the most outrageous thing to have developed in the first place,' Raven Smith said when we discussed this on the podcast. 'It's just barbaric. I think like anything, it's like an SEO thing that people just want to narrow their options because we have these infinite options at our fingertips, but it's actually just straight-up racist.'

Different studies have shed light on how different demographics experience racism on dating apps. Such as a recent Australian study, which looked specifically at how 'sexual racism', as they termed it, affected gay and bisexual Asian men.*

Here are some of the stories they heard from participants:

He says 'send me a picture of your face'. I send him a picture of my face, and he says 'oh you're an Indian. I'm sorry'. He then quickly blocked me. – James, 28, Indian

So many profiles had 'not into Asians', 'not into this [or that]' . . . I was just so confused as to why that was. I was skinny, young, cute, and I thought that would be enough – Rob, 27, Cambodian

I feel like the bad fruit that nobody wants. – Ted, 32, Vietnamese

---

* Gene Lim, Brady Robards, and Brownyn Carlson, *The Conversation*, July 2020.

In 2014, dating site and app OKCupid conducted a survey that found that heterosexual Asian men received the fewest number of messages from heterosexual women, while heterosexual black women received the fewest number of messages from heterosexual men.

The journalist Jessica Morgan has received messages from men on dating apps who have complimented her for being mixed race, as opposed to being 'fully black'. 'That just suggests that being black is shameful,' she told me, adding that she is frequently quizzed about her ethnicity on dating apps. 'Rather than be faced with overt racism, the messages I've received have been more backhanded and are subtle microaggressions,' she explained. 'They say things like, "I've never dated a black girl before", raising red flags of fetishisation, or "you're pretty for a black girl".' Morgan is also Jewish, which she states on her dating app profile. 'Some Jewish men have told me that despite being born to a Jewish mother, they would never date me because of the way I looked, and the fact that I was black,' she said. 'It is actually quite shocking how many messages like this I receive from mostly conservative Jews. As much as I am a fiend of dating, it can be quite traumatising if you match with the wrong person.'

In 2018, the author Stephanie Yeboah wrote a blog post titled 'Dating When Plus-Sized & Dark Skinned', which outlined some of the messages she had received from men on dating apps, including 'you look like a dominant black queen' and 'I have such a thing for chocolate'. Yeboah expanded on the issue in an interview with me for the *Independent*. 'Some [of these men] blatantly exclaim that they would want to be in a relationship [with me] to "get a taste of jungle fever" and to see whether black women are "as aggressive in bed as they've heard",' she said, before explaining why messages such as these, which some may wrongly interpret as complimentary, are so dehumanising. 'They suggest that black women are only good for one thing, and it goes back to previous ideologies of black people being compared to primates, as primal and feral, hyper-sexualised creatures. It's very hurtful.'

Writers Yomi Adegoke and Elizabeth Uviebiné explain why the racism that people experience on dating apps can be complex in their bestselling 2018 book, *Slay in Your Lane: The Black Girl Bible*, explaining how it is sometimes labelled 'positive racism'. When Uviebiné and Adegoke came on the podcast to discuss this further, Adegoke explained that she hadn't really used dating apps much. 'I'm quite hesitant to use [them] maybe because of the things I've heard other people have gone through,' she said. 'I've heard people being like, "Oh you know, I've always wanted to taste chocolate" but it's not something I can say I've personally experienced.' Uviebiné concurred: 'Most women are dubious of [dating apps] anyway, but as a black woman you feel even more cautious because the stories are very well known of how people can talk to you on there.'

While it's crucial to have conversations about the ways in which minorities experience racism on dating apps, it's equally important not to make anyone sound like a victim. 'We're not victims,' Uviebiné said. 'And it's important for us to have these discussions but also to make sure we don't leave it with, everything's shit for you.'

When I put this to Morgan, she explained that any discussion about racism will inevitably spark accusations of feigning victimhood. 'Personally, I don't ever consider myself as a victim in this context per se,' she added. 'Of course, in a wider context, if you have faced racism on dating apps, you have been targeted and are victimised by the oppressor. But we can't hide from the fact that people do have unconscious and conscious biases and are discriminatory in every area, including dating apps.'

Of course, the racism that people experience on dating apps is a reflection of the racism that people experience off them too. Prior to appearing on the podcast, Babalola tweeted that the dating scene for black women in London was 'atrocious'. I asked her to explain this tweet when she came on the podcast. 'Because of desirability politics and white supremacy,' she said. 'Black women are seen as the bottom of the pile basically. It goes back to history, when white women were seen as the pinnacle of femininity and black women were meant to be the antithesis of this. We're meant to be hyper-masculine, grotesque, beastly. And so those things are perpetuated in so many small ways. It's why when we watch TV, there's a dark skinned black woman that's painted as aggressive. We never see a black woman, especially on British TV, being cherished and loved. And if we do, I can almost guarantee it will not be a dark skinned black woman. I think the last show I remember on British TV showing a dark skinned black woman in love was *Noughts and Crosses*, and *Noughts and Crosses* is literally about race and is about racism and so that was a very conscious decision.'

So far, I've painted a fairly bleak picture of dating apps. But it's not all bad, I promise. For the LGBT+ community, for example, apps have made it far easier to meet people who identify with the gender or genders that they are attracted to.

Perhaps this is why dating app usage tends to be higher among sexual minorities than among those who are straight.* There are currently more than fifty gender options and nine sexualities to choose from on Tinder. On OkCupid, there's a feature that allows you to declare which pronouns you use on your profile, making it one of the first dating apps to tailor to non-binary people. Even on Bumble – an app whose USP, that the 'woman has to message first', was entrenched in heteronormativity – now gives users the option to choose from several different gender identities.

When Munroe Bergdorf came on the podcast, she explained how, as a pansexual transgender woman, the increasing inclusivity of dating apps has made her feel more comfortable in the dating world. 'For a lot of trans people, we need to come out every time we're dating somebody,' Bergdorf began. '[On apps] you can really be transparent about your identity and who you want to date because it stops the need to come out all the time. It also stops fetishism as well.' On a lot of dating apps, you can now search for people by orientation, which Bergdorf added is 'very important' because it allows people to filter out sexualities and genders that don't suit a person's preferences. It can also eliminate the risk of encountering transphobia or homophobia. 'For me, I don't really like to date men that identify as straight,' Bergdorf said. 'Just because so much of my identity is within the queer realm, so it's great that I can search for other pansexual people or other bisexual people

---

* Pew Research found that sexual minorities are twice as likely to use online dating compared to straight people. Available at: https://www.pewresearch.org/internet/2020/02/06/the-virtues-and-downsides-of-online-dating/

and it just narrows down the pool of people that are going to be compatible with me.'

Of course, people do fall in love after meeting on an app. While it has never happened to me, it's happened to plenty of my friends. The Pew Research Centre found that 12 per cent of people have married or been in a committed relationship with someone they met online. Meanwhile, a separate study found that 46 per cent of people know someone who's entered into a long-term partnership or marriage from online dating.

The producer and podcaster Rubina Pabani, co-host of BBC Asian Network's *Brown Girls Do It Too* podcast, explained how she recognises that dating apps can be 'trashy' but that they gave her the opportunity to meet men she never would have otherwise met. 'Hot guys that I would have thought were out of my league, weirdos who made me rethink what it means to be alive, and that special breed of man who treats you like he wants to colonise India again,' she teased. Pabani is engaged to someone she met on a dating app.

The author and journalist Elizabeth Day also met her partner on Hinge. But, as she explained when she came on the podcast, she almost didn't go on the date. 'I met him at a time when I was just done with dating apps,' she said. 'He was the first person to match with me. The morning I met him, I'd booked flights to LA thinking I was going to move there. I just thought, "there's nothing for me in London". I only went on the date because I thought I should. And then I walked in and I was like, "oh my god". Thank goodness I did.'

Dating apps have changed the way we date forever, and while we may not like it, we have to accept it. Users might have some of the worst dating experiences of their lives, but they also might have some of the best. In the spirit of optimism and, well, acceptance, given that dating apps aren't going anywhere any time soon, let's conclude with something Day said on the podcast about adapting to this new way of dating. Because while we can't change the way dating apps work, we can rethink our approach to using them. 'I think it's about reconfiguring our idea of romance,' said Day.

'Someone I went on a Bumble date with told me he thought he was always going to meet his [partner] in a meet-cute, like a romcom meet-cute where they'd be at some party and he'd trip over and spill wine on her shoes and they'd have this dazzling connection, and it would be a moment of pure coincidence. Obviously the dating app scene doesn't allow for that. But maybe it's romantic in its own way, because when you come to a dating app and you answer all the profile questions, you have to be clear about what you want and committed to who you are as a person. And maybe that in itself is kind of romantic if someone is drawn to that.'

Chapter Six
Cracking On and Mugging Off

When Curtis Pritchard dumped Amy Hart, I cried like he'd just dumped me. In fact, I sobbed. They were hot, globular tears – the kind that leave you feeling like you need to soak in a bath and then sleep for five months afterwards. The trouble is, I had never actually met Curtis or Amy. I didn't even know their last names at the time. All I knew about them was that they were contestants on ITV2's reality TV series *Love Island*, and that I was very invested in their relationship.

The premise of *Love Island* is simple: five men and five women are sent to a villa in Mallorca and told to fall in love. The feelings are febrile, and the furniture is fluorescent. After eight weeks of break-ups, reconciliations and surprise new arrivals, one winning couple is awarded £50,000. Inadvertent consolation prizes include millions of Instagram followers and a clothing line with a fast fashion brand. That makes the programme sound vapid and the people on it nothing more than avaricious hashtaggers. To be honest, it sort of is and they sort of are. But it's also one of the most visceral depictions of millennial relationships I've ever seen.

Which brings me back to why I cried when Curtis dumped Amy. You see, they 'coupled up' early on. He was the clumsy ballroom dancer with the cheesy grin. She was the gregarious

pageant-queen-turned-flight attendant that described herself as
the 'Bridget Jones' of her friendship group. Together, they were
straight out of a West End musical. After just a few weeks of
dating, they declared themselves 'half' boyfriend and 'half'
girlfriend. And even though no one knew what that meant, it
was still adorable. But, tragically, Curtis and Amy never made
it to 'full' status. And that is because of Casa Amor.

Casa Amor is the ultimate test for couples on *Love Island*.
Normally occurring about halfway through the series, Casa
Amor sees either the men or the women move temporarily
into a second villa, which is then filled with six new single
contestants of the opposite sex. Meanwhile, those back in the
original villa are also given six new single housemates. Casa
Amor usually lasts for four days, which is more than enough
time to see just how committed to their partners the Islanders
are, with many ditching them for someone new. It is survival
of the fittest, but with high-rise bikinis and fake tan.

The most frustrating – but perhaps least surprising – element
of Casa Amor is that it is usually the men in committed
couples whose heads are turned by someone new. Meanwhile,
the women dutifully snuggle together on the sofa to avoid
sharing a bed with any of the new men and talk about how
much they like their partners. This is sadly what happened to
Amy and Curtis. Because, while she was busy planning how
to tell Curtis she loved him, he was telling a *Vogue* Italia model
named Jourdan that she was 'clever' and 'stunning' and that
something was missing in his relationship with Amy. Then he
kissed her.

But here's the complicated bit: Jourdan didn't like Curtis.
She actually liked Danny and rejected Curtis so that he had no
choice but to re-couple with Amy, who, blissfully ignorant to

her half boyfriend's wandering eyes and lips, was thrilled. This made it all the more heart-breaking to see the look on Amy's face when she found out she was just Curtis's backup plan. 'I was coming back here to tell you I loved you,' she told him, stony-faced and pointy-fingered, only to collapse later in the arms of her friends, mascara streaming down her face.

The break-up came later, when Amy sat Curtis down like a schoolteacher and rattled off a list of pre-prepared questions she had for him, such as: 'what is the definition of exclusive?' She spoke plainly and firmly, determined not to show this man just how much he had hurt her. It was powerful stuff. Curtis insisted that he meant everything he said to Amy about how much he liked her but confessed he couldn't promise her something like this wouldn't happen again. I was gobsmacked – and so was Amy. 'How can you be like, "I want a future with you, I do see a future with you" to now saying that you don't want to be with me?' she said as her eyes watered, before calling him a compulsive liar and storming off in her stilettos. Amy quit the show a few days later, proving that this was no ordinary reality TV heartbreak. Her leaving speech reduced everyone to tears, including Curtis, even though he had already started flirting with someone else.

Love is often stranger than fiction, which is why it's perfect fodder for reality TV. But there's more to it than that. Consider how, in *Love Island*, the viewer is given unparalleled access to the romantic lives of its stars. We watch relationships unfold from start to finish. We see every single flutter and flirtation: first kisses, first fumbles and first fights. And we see all this from both perspectives. With Amy, for example, we watched as she pined for Curtis and fantasised about their future together. But we also saw how Curtis was simultaneously umming and erring about Amy and flirting hopelessly with Jourdan. The bottom line is that we knew that Amy was going to get her heart broken before she did. It was devastating but it was also excellent television.

Love Island gives us an omnipotent view of relationships. Imagine if we had that in real life. We wouldn't have to agonise over trying to figure out if someone wasn't interested because we'd just know. Break-ups would be far less painful because we'd see them coming. And there'd be no mind games, because you can't play them when you know exactly what the other person is thinking. That's what makes *Love Island*, and programmes like it, so wildly successful. They give us the kind of insight into relationships that we will always want but never have.

Reality TV shows about dating have always been a hit. Look at the British cult classic *Blind Date*, which launched in 1985 and saw a single person 'blindly' choose someone to date from a batch of contestants on the other side of a wall, who answered questions posed by the singleton. The programme was designed to test whether or not you could be attracted to someone without ever having seen them, a concept that it borrowed from the American programme, *The Dating Game*, which launched in the US in 1965. Since then, this format has been refreshed and repackaged for the modern era umpteen times. Today, reality programmes about dating can be divided into several categories. There are the cheesy ones that make us smile: think *First Dates* and *Take Me Out*. The trashy ones that make us cringe: *Celebs Go Dating*, *Dinner Date* and *Ex on the Beach*. The extreme ones that make us sympathise with the contestants: *90 Day Fiancé*,

Married at First Sight and *Eating with My Ex*. The bizarre
ones that make you wonder how on earth they were ever
commissioned: *Naked Attraction*, *Beauty and the Geek* and
Playing it Straight. And the American ones that are so absurd
they've even spawned fictional programmes based on how
they were made: *Millionaire Matchmaker*, *The Bachelor* and
The Bachelorette.

On the surface, each of these programmes is about love,
but what they are really about, of course, is entertainment.
Which is why they all have various problems – more on that
later – and why the genre has become so much more outrageous in recent years. Take *Love is Blind*, the hit Netflix series
that tests whether or not people can fall in love with someone
they have never seen in thirty-eight days and then has the
couple marry six weeks later. Fans obsessed over the curious
'pods' in which the cast speed-dated on either side of a wall,
soaked up every last earnest platitude ('I've found my soul
mate without ever seeing them'), and squeezed their thighs in
solidarity as couples who'd spent weeks fantasising about one
another were finally able to touch. The show was so popular
that Netflix even announced its viewing figures – thirty million
households – despite that being information it usually with-
holds.

A few months after *Love is Blind* aired, Netflix delivered
yet another extreme dating show: *Too Hot to Handle*. The
programme gathered a group of sex- and fame-hungry singles
from around the world in a sun-soaked villa – so far, so *Love
Island* – with the caveat that nobody was allowed to touch,
kiss or have sex. And anyone who broke the rules faced a
penalty which would reduce the group prize money that the
winners would split. It was like watching a group of horny

teenagers writhing around in imaginary chastity belts. Needless to say, it was a huge hit.

But let's go back to *Love Island*. It stands out from the crowd of similar shows and I'm going to spend the rest of this chapter explaining why, starting with some of my personal highlights from the show since it started in 2015.

1. When Olivia declared herself the 'Fuck Boy whisperer'.
2. When Belle shaved Anton's bum just a few days after meeting him.
3. When Kem told Chris he finally felt like himself again because he was wearing white trousers and red trainers.
4. When Marcel kept telling people he was in Blazin' Squad but that he didn't like to talk about it, and then kept telling more people that he was in Blazin' Squad.
5. When Kem tried to explain that he was bored in his relationship with the following analogy: 'Here's the thing. Like, obviously I fucking love hummus. But at the moment, what's been going on is, we've been getting that hummus with the olive in it and I just don't like the taste of it. What I'm thinking is: breadsticks, celery, carrot. Change it up.'
6. When Hayley asked what an aura was.
7. When Hayley asked if Brexit meant we wouldn't have any trees.
8. When Chris spelled Jason Statham's name 'Jason Staythumb'.
9. When Cara farted on Nathan.
10. When everyone had been arguing and Chris asked: 'Anyone want me to rap to lift the mood a little bit?'

The beauty of *Love Island* is that it combines the silly with the serious, often without even realising. Because while it has plenty of moments like the above, which is part of the appeal to its millions of viewers, it also teaches those viewers valuable lessons about the contentions that manifest in modern relationships. Take feminism, for example. The subject has arisen to one degree or another in several episodes as Islanders navigate gender roles, sometimes playing up to stereotypes and other times fighting against them. Occasionally, this dichotomy would drive couples apart. Consider Camilla Thurlow and Jonny Mitchell's almighty fall out in season three. The two, who were coupled up at the time, were talking about first dates, and how theirs might pan out.

Here's what happened:

Camilla: Would you pay?

Jonny: Would I pay? I always pay. I was with my ex for five years, I don't remember her paying for a thing.

Camilla: What?!

Jonny: She offered at first, but in the end she just stopped offering.

Camilla: Because you always pay?

Jonny: Of course, I always pay.

Camilla: My gosh. But surely at the beginning it's better to go halves because you don't know how it's going to pan out?

Jonny: No. I'd feel almost emasculated if a girl paid.

Camilla: Really?! God, I'd feel so awkward if I didn't pay half.

Jonny: No, I wouldn't LET you pay. No, honestly, I wouldn't. I'd find it really fucking awkward. You're a feminist, aren't you?

Camilla: Shouldn't we all be feminists? Surely you believe in equality.

Jonny: Oh, I believe in equality. But I feel like feminism believes almost in inequality. The majority of feminists, like REAL feminists, believe almost in, like, a slope towards them rather than towards men.

Camilla: I don't think it's that, but I think it's difficult for men to see that there have been several generations which have been preferential towards men. And therefore to redress the balance, there has to be in some way an active movement towards equality.

Jonny: Do women not have equality?

Camilla: Absolutely not.

Jonny: How so?

Camilla: I mean, really? . . . There are still, like, if you look at the number of females in high-powered jobs, high-level jobs, top-tier jobs—

Jonny: The Prime Minister's a woman.

Camilla: Sure, but how many other female MPs are there?

Jonny: I know, but it's not like it's a boys' club. I'm sure they just choose who's more qualified for the job. I'm not sure if it matters.

I was thrilled when I watched this conversation unfold. Obviously, it was incredibly frustrating to hear Camilla have to explain, very sweetly and patiently, that feminism did not mean hating men and throwing your burning bras on them. But seeing her do it on TV was invaluable. Jonny is far from the only person with these views. Hearing his hopeless defence – he might as well have said he was not a feminist but a humanist (an ideology that has absolutely nothing to do with equality) – against Camilla's educated explanation, will have resonated with a lot of people. And it had a lot of value. Because not only did it demonstrate how to talk about feminism with a partner who might not be as educated on the subject as you, it also showed how important it is to have those conversations. After watching that exchange, it became clear that someone like Camilla was never going to be happy with someone like Jonny. And vice versa. Partners don't need to have the same interests, the same backgrounds, or even the same politics. But the core values – for example, whether you think men and women should be equal and whether you feel comfortable calling that feminism – have to match up.

Feminism matters a lot when it comes to dating. It can define every action and exchange in a relationship, from how you pay for dates and what you talk about, to how you argue and how you have sex. All this is particularly relevant to those in heterosexual relationships, where the traditional male–female gender dynamics are at play. On the podcast, we spoke about how feminism affects the way couples have sex with activist and author Gina Martin and illustrator Flo Perry, a conversation that was inspired by Perry's book, *How to Have Feminist Sex*. As Perry explained, feminist sex is all about having the kind of sex you want to have as opposed to having the kind of sex you feel you ought to have. For women, it's about feeling empowered to say what you do and don't like in bed, which is something that not enough of us do. 'We're so scared of being single that once you have the boyfriend or the girlfriend, you don't think, "Is this the sex I want to be having?" You don't prioritise your own pleasure. I think a lot of women especially do that,' she said.

We touched on dating and feminism again when activist

and comedian Grace Campbell came on the podcast. Campbell explained that her boyfriend at the time was 'definitely' a feminist, but that she'd previously dated misogynists. 'There was someone that I dated for a while who was very honest about him being really unattracted by my ambition,' she said, adding how she once told this boyfriend, who she was with aged 19, that she had wanted to win a BAFTA by the time she was 30. 'He just said he found it quite vulgar when I spoke about what I wanted to do and where I wanted to get to. That didn't last, obviously.'

It's interesting how many people – namely, men – misunderstand what feminism means, particularly in the context of dating. When Jonny asks Camilla if she's a feminist ('you're a feminist, aren't you?'), he makes it sound a slur, as if 'feminist' was a word used to describe someone who might try and slice your dick off. But this way of thinking is systemic. Take the blog post on the now-defunct *Guardian* Soulmates dating service that was headlined 'How to date a feminist'. The article was clearly well-meaning, and possibly designed to help people like Jonny, who haven't the foggiest what feminism actually means. But its very existence undermined feminism itself by presenting it as some kind of exotic movement. The article, written in 2017, was also very patronising, and included advice such as 'give her time to speak' and 'avoid calling her "darling" or "babe"'.

How feminism intersects with dating is an important conversation. And *Love Island* raised it. Yes, the same show on which people play games like 'how well do you know your sex positions?' and 'who is the best balloon thruster?'. Here's another important topic of conversation the show raised: gaslighting. I'd heard the term before, thanks to a viral *Teen Vogue* article from 2016 by Lauren Duca titled 'Donald Trump is Gaslighting America', but I learned what it meant in the context of relationships thanks to *Love Island*. Gaslighting is a form of psychological manipulation in which a person makes someone question their own perception of reality. It's a form of emotional abuse, and it's extremely common in cases of domestic violence, when abusive partners can cause victims to question their own sanity as a means of asserting control over them. But gaslighting can manifest in subtle ways, as we saw several times on *Love Island*.

In 2018, there was a contestant on the show called Adam Collard who had coupled up with a woman named Rosie Williams. Adam had already developed a reputation as someone who didn't respect women's boundaries – when one contestant rejected his advances to spoon in bed, he asked for a kiss instead, telling her: 'so we don't have to spoon when we get back'. But the drama with Rosie started when he called her materialistic to several other Islanders behind her back. Rosie, meanwhile, was still under the impression that she and Adam had been getting along just fine, so was understandably rather taken aback when it was relayed to her what Adam had been saying. Rosie confronted Adam in front of everyone, telling him that what he'd done was 'bang out of order' and that he should have come to her first if he had doubts about their relationship. It was pretty empowering viewing, with Rosie telling another Islander why she wanted to confront Adam publicly beforehand: 'I'm not just doing this for me. I'm doing it for every girl who's been played by a playboy.' Adam showed little remorse, but ultimately apologised and the two soon reconciled. Then, a new woman entered the villa, Zara McDermott, and Adam was interested. He spent the next few days flirting with Zara and ignoring Rosie, except for the night when Rosie gave him a hand job.

When Rosie confronted Adam this time around – 'you've literally just had what you wanted and ditched me one hour later' – he refused to accept any responsibility. In fact, he gave her a Cheshire cat smile, called her 'ass-y' and said her reaction was 'funny'. The exchange prompted hundreds of tweets describing Adam's behaviour as 'abusive' and 'manipulative'. Ofcom even received complaints from twenty-one members of the public. The morning after the episode aired, Women's Aid, a national charity working to end domestic violence against women, issued a statement that accused Adam of gaslighting Rosie. 'On the latest series of *Love Island*, there are clear warning signs in Adam's behaviour,' it began.

> In a relationship, a partner questioning your memory of events, trivialising your thoughts or feelings, and turning things around to blame you can be part of a pattern of gaslighting and emotional abuse. Last night, Rosie called out Adam's unacceptable behaviour on the show. We ask viewers to join her in recognising unhealthy behaviour in relationships and speaking out against all forms of domestic abuse – emotional as well as physical. It is only when we make a stand together against abuse in relationships that we will see attitudes change and an end to domestic abuse.

The incident spawned multiple articles, Twitter threads and discussions on daytime television about gaslighting and what it meant. It felt like everyone was familiarising themselves with the term for the first time. And that was thanks to *Love Island*. The programme has continued to raise conversations about gaslighting since. Like in the following series, when Joe Garratt questioned his partner Lucie Donlan over her friendship with fellow contestant Tommy Fury, calling it 'strange' and 'disrespectful'. Lucie insisted that she and Tommy were just friends and that there was nothing romantic between them. To which Joe said: 'I think it's time for you to get close with the girls.'

More than 1,000 viewers complained to Ofcom following the episode, while Twitter lit up with people accusing Joe of controlling behaviour. Once again, Women's Aid weighed in with a statement praising viewers for recognising Joe's behaviour. 'Controlling behaviour is never acceptable, and with *Love Island* viewers complaining to Ofcom in record numbers about Joe's possessive behaviour towards Lucie, more people are becoming aware of this and want to challenge it,' the charity said. 'Abusive relationships often start off with subtle signs of control, so it's important that it is recognised at an early stage. *Love Island* viewers are now very vocal in calling out unhealthy behaviour between couples on the show, and this is a positive development.'

In the sixth season, Connor Durman was accused of 'controlling' his partner Sophie Piper. And back in season three, after he questioned the value of feminism, Jonny was called out by Women's Aid for saying that newcomer Theo Campbell would have to 'prise [Tyla Carr, his then love interest] from his cold dead hands' if Theo expressed an interest in her. 'We commented that this was not romantic banter but signalled that this man believes he owns this woman,' said Laura Dix, national community engagement manager at Women's Aid. Dix explained that the programme had been hugely helpful in terms of shedding light on emotional abuse.

'Manipulative and possessive behaviour can look obvious on the screen, and it is a positive development that *Love Island* viewers were so vocal in calling out unhealthy relationship behaviour between couples,' she told me. 'In this way, survivors of domestic abuse can learn to recognise behaviour intended to demean, denigrate, confuse and control them. It is only when we make a stand together against abuse in relationships that we will see attitudes change and an end to domestic abuse.'

Another issue that was not part of the PSHE syllabus at school but comes up time and time again on *Love Island* is the way that we view female sexuality. Popular culture has long perpetuated the idea of womanhood as a binary identity. By that, I mean that women have traditionally been represented in films, TV shows and music as either 'good' or 'bad', and whichever label they accrue depends on their sexual behaviour. The 'good' girl is virginal while the 'bad' girl is sexually active and therefore seen as promiscuous. This is often referred to as the Madonna–Whore dichotomy; the former being something women are told to aspire towards, while the latter is something they must circumvent. It's the name attached to a complex first identified by Sigmund Freud in which someone is unable to maintain sexual arousal within a committed relationship, the idea being that love and desire are mutually exclusive.

This concept actually dates back to the beginning of time. As Harry Benshoff wrote in *Film and Television Analysis: An Introduction to Methods, Theories, and Approaches*, 'this split is central to Western culture and Christianity', with Eve viewed as the original 'bad' girl for giving into temptation in the Garden of Eden. Simplifying femininity in this way benefits the patriarchy because it reinforces gender roles that reduce women to caricatures and therefore enables men to be viewed as three-dimensional, thus giving them more agency. What it also does is imply that women who have sexual autonomy – 'bad' girls like Eve – are something to be feared.

You will have seen the Madonna–Whore dichotomy at work either in popular culture or in real life. Perhaps it was the time you heard a friend call someone a slut because they slept with two people in the same evening. Or the time you heard someone make assumptions about a woman's sexual history based on the way she dressed. If you've watched *Love Island*, you'll have seen it manifest to an almost hyperbolic degree. Amelia Morris explores this subject in her research paper, 'Good Girls VS Bad Girls: exploring the representations of female sexuality on ITV's *Love Island*'. She points to the frequency with which male contestants refer to female contestants as 'wifey material' and say things such as 'I could introduce her to my mum'. This way of speaking, Morris argues, 'categorizes the female contestants into good vs bad, the suggestion being that one "type" of woman would be welcomed into a family environment, whilst another is reserved only for fulfilling sexual gratification.'

There are 'good girls' and 'bad girls' in every season of *Love Island*. The good ones are sweet-natured, smiley and approachable – think Dani Dyer (season four) and, well, Amy Hart (season five) – and they almost always join the show at the beginning. This is a clever strategy, one that helps facilitate the good–bad girl dichotomy because viewers have more time to get to know these original cast members and so will be more likely to root for their success over contestants who join later, such as the bad girls. These 'bad girls' are crafty, crude and most importantly, very fucking horny – they are the ones you'll see talking about sex the most. They usually enter midway through, all slow-motion and skimpy swimwear. Employed as agents of sexual chaos, the bad girls do not tend to befriend the other women in the villa because they are too busy thinking about dick.

One of *Love Island*'s most notorious bad girls was Megan Barton-Hanson (season four). This was not just because of the way she looked (cushion lips and surgically enhanced breasts) or the way she behaved (she made a move on one contestant when he was already coupled up) but because prior to appearing on the show, Barton-Hanson had worked as a stripper. These ingredients combined to create the ultimate bad girl cocktail. You see, there's a lot of stigma attached to sex work, and we saw this frequently manifest on the show with regards to Barton-Hanson. Consider the episode when, during a lie detector challenge, Barton-Hanson asked her partner, Wes Nelson, if he would feel embarrassed to introduce her to his family because of her career in sex work. Nelson insisted that he wouldn't, but the lie detector indicated he was lying. When I interviewed Barton-Hanson on the podcast, she told me that she was asked by a producer to ask that question. 'I knew I'd be portrayed as the maneater,' she said, before going on to explain where she thinks the stigma attached to sex workers stems from. 'I think it's just years and years being ingrained to people that it's shameful for women to actually use their body to benefit them,' she said before revealing how she'd been slut-shamed since school. 'It made me more stubborn to go into [the sex industry] and be like, I've got that label anyway, I'm going to take control of [it].'

There's one task on *Love Island* that happens every season, and it always separates the bad girls from the good. It's the Mr and Mrs challenge, when coupled-up Islanders have to guess random facts about their partner, including how many people they've slept with. Good girls have low numbers, bad girls have high ones. When Barton-Hanson revealed she'd slept with twenty men on the programme, Twitter users accused her of lying about her age (24) because that seemed like too high a number.

Because that's the thing, women *aren't* allowed to enjoy sex. At least not in the same way men are. That's what makes them bad girls. Look at the reaction to Barton-Hanson's fellow contestant Adam Collard revealing he'd slept with 200 women in the Mr and Mrs Challenge – there wasn't one. Not really, anyway. Or how Marcel Somerville from the 2017 season was met with laughter and jokes from fellow contestants when he revealed he'd slept with 'around' 300 women.

Reducing women to either bad or good girls on *Love Island* might be frustrating, but it makes sense. Yes, it is a reality TV show, but it borrows elements from fictional narratives in order to ramp up the entertainment, such as perpetuating this idea of two-dimensional characters. This is achieved in a number of ways, including careful editing and manipulative producing, e.g. the producer telling Barton-Hanson to ask Nelson that question about introducing her to his family as a former stripper, something that adds to her 'bad girl' narrative. Barton-Hanson has not watched herself on the series, but through the media attention she received and the kind of DMs she gets sent (a lot of which are slut-shaming comments), she told me that she feels like she was misrepresented. 'There's a hint of me in there but it's been amplified massively,' she said. 'It was me, but the situations they put me in and the

way they edited it down wasn't me. It would have been nicer
if they showed other sides of my personality as well.' The
25-year-old described herself to me as 'quite goofy' and
lamented that none of her sense of humour seemed to have
come across on the show. 'That's one of the reasons I've never
watched it back,' she said. 'Because in my head it was a lovely
experience and I don't want to tarnish it by seeing how they
edited it and how I came across.'

Let's look at another one of *Love Island*'s bad girls: Maura
Higgins from season five. Almost every clip of the Irish then-
28-year-old showed her talking about sex. Like Barton-Hanson
before her, Higgins's horniness showed no regard for the usual
codes of conduct; she was often seen flirting with men who
were already in couples and purported to get 'fanny flutters'
from almost anyone. *Vice*'s Emma Garland described her as an
'Irish Samantha Jones'. Occasionally, Maura took things too
far. Like when she insisted on kissing Tommy Fury on the
sofa after he'd already rebuffed her advances, an incident that
prompted more than 480 complaints to Ofcom.

Because Higgins was characterised as a bad girl from the
second she strutted into the villa, people made assumptions
about her sex life. They assumed that because she spoke about
sex all the time, she must have bedded hundreds of men. In
fact, at the time of the show, Higgins had only slept with six
people, something that shocked her fellow Islanders. Higgins
defied her characterisation as a bad girl again later in the series,
when she and partner Tom Walker were given the opportunity
to sleep in The Hideaway – a place in the villa where they
could spend the night alone as opposed to in a bed surrounded
by their castmates. Fellow Islander Molly-Mae Hague told
Higgins, 'You're definitely going to have sex tonight, aren't

you?' to which Higgins replied, 'I'm not going to, no!' Another of the women said, 'Oh come on you've given it all of this now you've got to follow through,' implying that, as Higgins had spoken about sex so much, she'd obviously want to jump at the first opportunity to copulate. But she didn't and insisted that she'd only kissed Walker three times. Then, just before they went to The Hideaway, Higgins overheard Walker talking about her to the other men. 'It will be interesting to know if she's all mouth or not,' Walker told them. Higgins called him out for being disrespectful and told the other girls that she wanted a 'gentleman' rather than a 'lad'. She later asked: 'We're in 2019, why is it such a big deal when a girl talks about sex?'

Men aren't the only ones who subscribe to the Madonna–Whore dichotomy. It is unfortunately so entrenched in our society, that women do it too, often without realising. Take Zara Holland from season three, a former Miss Great Britain winner, who was stripped of her title for having sex with Alex Bowen on the programme because Miss GB could no longer 'promote Zara as a positive role model' – another painful reminder of how shamefully society views female sexuality. Holland confided in fellow contestant Kady McDermott afterwards, making her promise not to tell anyone. But McDermott immediately told the other Islanders, calling Holland a 'stupid girl' while another contestant, Olivia Buckland, teased: 'Miss GB fucks on the first date, you sure?' Morris examines this exchange in her research paper, writing: 'Here, Zara's reputation as a pageant queen – historically presented as "pure" and "virginal" – is juxtaposed with her "bad" sexual behaviours, positioning her as possessing contradictory characteristics of both "Madonna" and "whore".' The fact that the other Islanders couldn't accept this contradiction shows how female sexuality is so frequently only understood in binary terms. But it also shows us something else.

Internalised misogyny is when women subconsciously project signs of sexism onto themselves and other women. It is systemic, but it is also so entrenched that it often goes unnoticed. The conversation about Holland is an obvious example. A less obvious, but no less important, one was Barton-Hanson's reaction when, during a Mr and Mrs challenge, her partner, Eyal Booker, guessed that she'd slept with 37 people, rather than the actual number of 20. She was furious. 'I'm not the most innocent of girls, but it doesn't mean that I've gone around shagging everyone I can,' she said afterwards in a piece to camera. 'I was absolutely fuming. Just because I'm open and I say I enjoy sex, it's 2018. I'm a woman. I'm allowed to enjoy sex if I want to, but it doesn't mean that I've slept with every Tom, Dick and Harry that walks in a bar.' Barton Hanson's defensiveness here illustrated the extent to which women can internalise a fear being labelled a 'bad girl'. Higgins showed signs of this too when she vowed to talk about sex a bit less on the show because, as she put it, 'maybe boys don't like that'.

We spoke about some of the ways internalised misogyny manifests in relationships more generally on the podcast with Florence Given. In her book *Women Don't Owe You Pretty*, Given explains how women often feel hostile towards a partner's ex-girlfriend. 'Internalised misogyny is when you put yourself in competition with a woman,' she explained. 'And we do that with most women we interact with unless we consciously tell ourselves not to. So, when you're with a partner and they have an ex that is a woman, you literally put yourself in competition with that woman because you want to be better, you want to be what that partner never was for your current partner, you want to not make the same mistakes.'

Both Given and I confessed to being guilty of internalised misogyny ourselves. 'I used to slut-shame my friends internally,' she said. 'I'd never call them a slut, but because of all of these messages I've been fed about women, I'd think they were easy.' One insult commonly used to slut-shame women is that they have 'loose' vaginas. The idea is that in women who have slept with multiple men, their vagina loses its tightness, rendering sex less pleasurable for their male partners. As a result, they are viewed as less desirable. This theory makes zero sense, as Given explained: 'I read this thing, I think it was a tweet that said it's interesting how men think that a woman who sleeps with thirty different guys has a loose vagina but a woman who has a boyfriend and has fucked him so many times is all of a sudden like not under the same category.' The 'loose vagina' jibe also ignores the fact that vaginal tightness can actually be a sign of an STD, or even vaginismus, a condition which means that sex is incredibly painful and distressing. Therefore, being 'loose' is, in many cases, much better.

My internalised misogyny was less about slut-shaming and more about pitting myself against other women, specifically my then-partner's ex-girlfriends. I explained in Chapter Four how, when we first started dating, I would stalk them all on social media with minute precision, comparing myself to every part of them and trying to find ways to make myself feel superior. I would do this by pigeonholing each of these women and saying things to myself like, 'she's trying to be edgy' and 'she thinks she's better than everyone else', when really I was the one trying to convince myself that I was better than them.

Educational though it may be, there are a lot of problems with *Love Island*. Its heteronormative format informs the contestants' conversations to the degree that occasionally, moments of homophobia slip through. Take the time when Higgins said that she had been with a girl once, before swiftly reassuring everyone that she was '100 per cent into men, but it just happened'. A similar thing happened in the second season of the show when there was a brief romance between Sophie Gradon and Katie Salmon. Gradon later downplayed the dalliance, claiming she had been 'faking' it in order to stay on the programme.

Barton-Hanson has come out as bisexual since leaving *Love Island*, revealing that she was originally rejected for the show after telling the producers that she was 'more into girls'. 'I don't think the sole reason they didn't let me on was because I was interested in women,' Barton-Hanson told me, revealing how, in her initial interview, she also said that the typical *Love Island* man wasn't her type. 'I was very fussy so they probably thought, "oh god, she's going to be hard work."' The next year, Barton-Hanson reapplied, partly because she wanted to move away from stripping. This time, she didn't mention that she was interested in women. She was immediately cast.

During her time on the show, Barton-Hanson didn't mention her bisexuality. I asked if she regretted not bringing it up. She said that she did, but that she kept it secret intentionally due to fear that discussing it would add to her characterisation as promiscuous. This is a symptom of biphobia and taps into the stereotype that suggests bisexual people are somehow more licentious. In other words, Barton-Hanson didn't want to be seen as a badder bad girl. 'I didn't want to add to that by being like, oh I like girls too,' she said. 'It took me so long to come out because I work in the sex industry, I didn't want [my bisexuality] to be for the male gaze or for people to think, "oh she's doing it for attention" or to seem more appealing to men. That is the furthest thing from the truth. So that's why I kept it so quiet.' It wasn't until Barton-Hanson went on a different reality TV show, *Celebs Go Dating*, that she came out as bi.

It's not clear whether *Love Island* will ever become more sexually diverse, but it doesn't look likely to happen soon. Despite the fact that half of *Love Island* fans have said they would watch a same-sex version of the show and prominent figures in the LGBT+ community, including Years and Years frontman Olly Alexander, have called for just that, ITV executives have shut down the idea.* 'The format doesn't really allow it,' said ITV boss Paul Mortimer in response to the demands. Producer Richard Cowles added: 'For a dating show, you need everyone to fancy everyone,' he said, 'so if you have gay and heterosexual in the same place, they're not going to fancy each other.' Cowles later said that he would consider a queer version of the show 'for a gay audience with a gay villa'. But just how helpful would that be? And wouldn't it simply marginalise the LGBT+ community further by ostracising them from the 'main' show by creating an entirely different spin-off? As writer Alexandra Pollard put it in the *Independent*,

---

* YouGov, January 2020. Available at: https://yougov.co.uk/topics/entertainment/articles-reports/2020/01/10/half-love-island-fans-would-watch-same-sex-series-

if Cowles wants everyone to fancy everyone, 'surely your best chances of having that happen are to fill the villa with queer people? When the question of LGBT+ representation comes up, there is a lot of bluster about logistics and formatting issues. But with a few small tweaks, they could just allow anyone, of any sexuality, to enter the villa, and then let them couple-up with whoever they want. Simple.'

Another complaint that comes up on every season of *Love Island* is that of body image. Everyone looks the same: slim, impossibly toned and well-groomed. The teeth are always white, the skin is always flawless and the lips are almost always big. It's hard not to pass judgement on the contestants' bodies, considering the cast spend 95 per cent of their time on the show in swimwear. Even the programme's late host, Caroline Flack, once admitted that *Love Island* portrayed 'unrealistic body standards'.

According to a survey of 4,505 adults carried out by YouGov in 2019, almost one in four people aged between 18 to 24 say that watching reality television makes them feel worried about their bodies. The findings led many to point the finger at *Love Island*, with Dr Antonis Kousoulis, a director at the Mental Health Foundation across England and Wales (which commissioned the research), criticising the show for projecting a body image that is 'not diverse, largely unrealistic and presented as aspirational'.

In 2017, *Love Island* was accused of sparking a four-fold surge in steroid usage among male viewers due to the overly muscular bodies of so many of the male contestants. Meanwhile, former contestant Simon Searles claimed that some of the male Islanders in his season became so consumed with the appearance of their bodies that they refused to eat carbohydrates. They also worked out 'like crazy' to maintain their physiques, he said.

Then there is the matter of plastic surgery. It is a well-known fact that a lot of *Love Island* contestants have gone under the knife. And while there is of course nothing wrong with that, it becomes problematic when a show that puts so much emphasis on the way people look is full of faces and bodies that have been surgically enhanced. Not only because it inadvertently aligns plastic surgery with body confidence, but also because it implies that people who don't have a spare £20,000 to mould their face into a Snapchat filter aren't worthy of love. It didn't help that advertisements for cosmetic surgery used to run during the ad breaks when *Love Island* aired, something that led the Mental Health Foundation to complain to the Advertising Standards Authority (ASA). The charity argued that the ads 'exploited young women's insecurities' and 'trivialised' breast enhancement surgery.

But solving *Love Island*'s body diversity issue is not quite as simple as casting people with bigger, and less chiselled, bodies. The writer Sofie Hagen argued on a recent podcast that, as a fat woman, she didn't actually want to see fat people on the show because seeing them be rejected in favour of slimmer contestants would actually be more damaging and make the show difficult and unpleasant to watch. Writer Zing Tsjeng agreed with Hagen in regards to East Asian representation. Her argument was hypothetical considering there has never been an East Asian *Love Island* contestant. Yomi Adegoke, who was on the same podcast, agreed that this also reflected how she felt about the lack of black women on the programme.

Samira Mighty was the first black woman to appear on

Love Island – and that was in 2018, three years after the show started. The following year, there was, once again, just one black woman cast: Yewande Biala. But their inclusion was described as 'bittersweet' by Adegoke. Both Biala and Mighty had a tough time with the men on the show and were often seen lamenting the fact that they were not someone's 'type on paper', as is so often the parlance of the programme. But, as Adegoke astutely put it in an article for British *Vogue*: 'It's hard to be black when the check boxes on that paper are usually "blonde" or "brunette".'

None of these issues are only relevant to *Love Island*. The other reality TV programmes I mentioned earlier all suffer the same setbacks. Body diversity is a problem across the board, as is sexual and racial diversity. Take *The Bachelor*, which has been running since 2002. The programme sees one man select a wife from a pool of single women, who figuratively (and sometimes literally) battle it out for his affection. It wasn't until June 2020 – shortly after the Black Lives Matter protests and eighteen years since the show first aired – that the programme cast its first black Bachelor.

Of course, we must also consider how this all impacts mental health, a subject that carries particular weight with regards to discussions surrounding *Love Island*, given that two former contestants – Mike Thalassitis and Sophie Gradon – have taken their own lives since appearing on the show. Additionally, many former contestants have spoken out about experiencing mental health issues since appearing on the programme, including Malin Andersson, Alex Miller and Zara Holland, who has spoken about seeking psychological help after a stint on the show in 2016. 'When I sat down and talked to [the therapists] together we pulled out the target points that triggered everything off and unfortunately that was from going on *Love Island*,' Holland told the BBC in 2018. As for specific triggers, former contestants have pointed to the difficulties of experiencing sudden fame, having their personal lives eviscerated in the tabloids, the pressure to stay relevant and not receiving sufficient aftercare from production – something that ITV2 has worked hard to rectify with a revamped fourteen-month-long duty of care programme. All this combined with the shocking death of Caroline Flack, who hosted the show for four years and died by suicide in 2020, prompted many people to call for *Love Island* to be cancelled altogether.

Love Island should be airing as I write this book, but isn't because of coronavirus. Even if it was, though, I'm not sure how many people would be watching. The most recent season aired in January 2020, the plan being that two seasons would then air each year: one in winter, filmed in South Africa, and one in summer, filmed in Mallorca. But the inaugural winter series was a flop. Critics asked why we needed two seasons a year of *Love Island* and it seemed that viewers agreed given that viewing figures for the opening episode were down by 800,000 compared to that of the preceding series.

Then there is the argument that, as *Love Island* has grown in popularity, it has become less about people finding love and more about them finding fame. Many of the most recent cast members already have substantial Instagram followings prior to entering the villa and are approached by producers as opposed to applying themselves. Their motivations are commercial rather than romantic, and it's glaringly obvious to the viewer. Gone are the endearing friendship dynamics and the genuine relationships – Camilla Thurlow and Jamie Jewitt are the last couple from the show to have stayed together for longer than a year; they appeared in the 2018 season.* Even Dani Dyer and Jack Fincham, whose relationship stole the hearts of millions when they won the show in 2019, didn't last beyond ten months. When I interviewed Dyer on the podcast, she explained how the media attention she and Fincham received when they left the programme made it difficult to sustain a relationship. 'The more you say, the more it gets twisted,' she said. 'Everyone's going to have an opinion, everyone's going to assume stuff and everyone's going to read things.'

For Barton-Hanson, who split from Nelson after just six months, it was a matter of having different priorities. 'He was very career-driven, taking every job under the sun and rightly so. But because I'd already experienced having money fairly easy with the stripping, I was more dedicated and focused on the relationship,' she told me. 'So it's super hard to get that balance just right and work together.'

It's not surprising that most relationships from the show fail. Think about it. You spend eight weeks living a life that is completely – and ironically – devoid of reality. There's no technology, no responsibility, there aren't even any clocks. When I interviewed former Islander Montana Brown on the podcast, she said they were even sometimes asked to change the subject of their conversations if they were deemed 'too boring'. It's a completely unnatural environment in which to

---

* Molly-Mae Hague and Tommy Fury have also now passed this benchmark, having been together since they were runners up on the 2019 series.

live, let alone fall in love. So, it's no surprise that this has a negative impact on contestants.

'The pressure was insane,' recalled Barton-Hanson. 'I think it's kind of unhealthy in a way because it's just not normal. You have no outside influences, you have no bills to pay, you have no phones. You have no distractions.' And that's just when you're on the programme, when you come off it, chances are your life will be completely unrecognisable to what it was before. 'Obviously you've been given this wonderful platform with so many Instagram followers and so many wonderful opportunities ahead of you, but unless you're completely in sync [with your partner] and you want the same things, it's never going to work.'

If *Love Island* does return to our screens, it will need to undergo a radical transformation in order to stay relevant. The fun of the programme is that it holds up a mirror to our culture, reflecting the very best and the very worst parts of how people behave in relationships. But the view needs to widen, because muscular straight people aren't the only ones who fall in love, and people have finally tired of seeing that on their screens. I really hope it does return, though, in a new, diversified format, because to lose a show that so seamlessly blends the serious with the spurious would be a grave shame. It would also be a missed opportunity for people like me, who were not taught about things such as gaslighting, female sexuality and internalised misogyny in school, but can learn what they mean – and address them – by sinking into their sofa and turning on ITV2 every evening for eight weeks straight. Without that, we'd be forced to learn about these things the hard way. I know what I'd prefer.

Chapter Seven
X-Rated

The first time I watched porn, I was fascinated. I had arrived at a friend's house to find a group of fellow 15-year-old girls huddled around the TV, watching a blonde woman spitting on one penis while a second one pounded her from behind. She was moaning; the men were grunting like a pair of hungry walruses. So this is sex, I thought. Fuck. We sat there for hours, pummelled into silence as the scenes became more and more extreme. Young women yelling 'daddy' as older men slapped their smooth derrières. People sitting on each other's faces and moaning in pleasure. Gangbangs. Blowbacks. Orgies. We watched all of it. And then we ate Hula Hoops.

Most people are exposed to porn before they have sex. A recent report from the British Board of Film and Classification found that some children watch it for the first time from as young as 7 years old, with the majority doing so between the ages of 11 and 13.* But most people don't lose their virginity until they're over the age of 16, which is the legal age for consent in the UK. So, there's a significant gap there, one that could shape the way you think and feel about sex for years.

---

* Available at: https://www.bbfc.co.uk/about-bbfc/media-centre/children-see-pornography-young-seven-new-report-finds

Porn has existed in one form or another for centuries. But millennials came of age as the industry was riding the wave of the dot-com boom; when pornographic content suddenly became more accessible than ever before. Naked bodies weren't just on VHS or in *Playboy*. They were online – and they were very easy to find. Pictures became videos and videos became streamable films. Soon, all of it was free. Today, mainstream porn is primarily consumed on 'tube websites': Xtube, YouPorn, RedTube and the one that rules them all, Pornhub, which launched in 2007. In 2019, Pornhub reported over forty-two billion visits to its site in total, with an average of 115 million visits a day. To put that into perspective, that's the size of the populations of Canada, Australia, Poland and the Netherlands *combined*.

The sheer volume and variety of porn available on these websites is astonishing. There are filters to suit any sexual predilection and fetish you can think of, from 'babysitter' to 'cartoon'. As the famous Rule 34 of the Internet Rules meme states: if it exists, there is porn of it. And yet, despite how wide-ranging the videos on Pornhub and co. are, when we talk about porn, we tend to focus on one very specific type. The bad type. The type that equates violence with sexual intensity, degrades women and presents them as sexual objects that are to be consumed through a misogynist, and sometimes racist, lens. These scenes are not about sex, but about fucking. The distinction being that there is a lack of intimacy, love, respect and sometimes even consent. This is the porn my friends and I grew up watching and hearing about without any understanding of how it differed from real-life sex. This is partly because of a wider societal taboo that inhibits honest conversations around sex, but it's mostly because of the UK's embarrassingly backwards approach to sex education. Did you know it was actually illegal for teachers to even talk to children about homosexuality until 2003?* And that sex education wasn't compulsory in all UK schools until 2020? And that before then, the syllabus hadn't been updated in 17 years? There was no requirement for children to be taught about cybersex, LGBT+ issues, consent, masturbation, nothing. Sex was simply something you did to get pregnant, at least that's what school told us – in addition to how to put a condom on a banana, of course.

My friends and I didn't speak about sex, either. Not in a way that was worthwhile or helpful, anyway. Obviously it was a big deal when someone lost their virginity, and while we would profess to wanting to know 'every last dirty detail', all that usually meant was which positions you did, how long it lasted and if someone's penis curved to the left or the right. We didn't talk about anything meaningful. And so, if we wanted to know more about sex, we would turn to porn, which is perhaps why we were all so captivated by that video tape.

I didn't watch a lot of porn growing up. But that doesn't mean my view of sex was not shaped by it. How could it not be, when I've been slapped, choked and had my hair pulled painfully hard during sex, all without my consent or direction? Yes, those men might have picked up those habits from other partners, but they're all rife in porn, which makes it difficult not to see a link. None of those actions made me

---

* This is because of Section 28, a controversial law that prevented schools in the UK from presenting homosexuality as a viable sexual orientation.

feel comfortable, but I let them happen because I thought that's what everyone else was doing. It took being in a long-term relationship at the age of 24 to realise that sex didn't have to be like that. It was supposed to feel good. Great, in fact. And for both of you. No one had ever told me that when I was growing up.

'There's an entire generation growing up that believes that what you see in hardcore pornography is the way that you have sex,' said social sex pioneer Cindy Gallop in her viral TED talk from 2009. Gallop explained how she realised this herself after sleeping with a number of men in their twenties who asked her to do things during sex that clearly came from porn. 'I have no problem responding as I have regularly had to, "actually no thank you very much, I'd rather you did not come on my face",' Gallop said. 'My concern is particularly with the young girl whose boyfriend wants to come on her face, she does not want him to come on her face. But hardcore porn has taught her that all men love coming on women's faces, all women love having their faces come on, and therefore she must let him come on her face, and she must pretend to like it.' Gallop later proudly said it was the first time the phrase 'come on her face' had been heard so many times on the TED stage.

That TED talk saw Gallop unveil her revolutionary social sex website Make Love Not Porn, which was launched as a way of highlighting the damaging misconceptions people have about sex thanks to porn. The website did this by listing comparisons between what happens during sex in the porn world versus the real world.

Here's an example she showed the audience during her TED talk:

> *Porn world: Women come all the time in positions where*
>   *nothing is going on anywhere near the clit.*
> *Real world: There has to be some sort of rhythmic pressure*
>   *on the clit in just the right way to make a woman come.*
>   *Can be pubic bone, tongue, fingers, or something else*
>   *entirely. But it has to be there.*

Sadly, I did not know about Gallop's website when I was a teenager. And I really wish I had, because maybe then I wouldn't have had to wait until I was 19 to have my first orgasm, courtesy of a vibrator that a friend bought me for Christmas. Female masturbation was shrouded in stigma when I was at school. There are many reasons for this – popular culture has traditionally normalised masturbation for men and stigmatised it for women – and porn is one of them. In porn, women come a lot. And in straight sex scenes in particular, they seem to do so without any stimulation whatsoever. A man's mere physical presence is enough to make them wet their knickers. In fact, it sometimes looks and sounds like they're coming just from simply giving a blow job – an idea that was both parodied and perpetuated by the seminal 1972 porn film *Deep Throat,* in which Linda Lovelace played a woman whose clitoris was located in her throat.

Female pleasure is almost never taken seriously in conventional porn. It's not even really considered at all. A 2017 study in the *Journal of Sex Research* found that in the fifty most-viewed Pornhub videos of all time, only 18 per cent included visual or verbal cues showing female pleasure, compared to 78 per cent showing male pleasure. It seems like too much of a coincidence, then, that female pleasure is seldom taken seriously in society, too. Scarlett Curtis spoke about this when she came on the podcast to discuss her Girls Wank Too campaign, which was launched as a way to demystify some of the taboos around female masturbation in the hope of empowering women to pleasure themselves free from shame. 'I started masturbating as a teenager like so many women do,' Curtis said. 'When I did start, I genuinely thought I was evil. Like I thought it was a sign there was something wrong with me. When I did it, I was like "never again. That was the last time, it's so gross."'

Curtis explained how she and so many of her other female friends felt like they'd invented masturbation because it wasn't something they ever spoke about to one another. The aim of her campaign was simply to encourage women to talk about masturbation, because that's the only way you tackle the taboo and empower women to start pleasuring themselves to the extent that they can learn what they like in bed. This is integral to good sex, because if you don't know what you're into, how can you possibly relay this to a partner? I learned this the hard way when, in my early twenties, a guy I was about to have sex with asked me what I 'liked'. I froze. What I liked was being alone in bed with my vibrator. 'I don't know,' I mumbled. Ten minutes later, he was going down on me. It did not feel good – sort of like a slug was slithering around digging for treasure – but I was too embarrassed to say anything. So I just let him get on with it while I thought about what I needed to buy from Sainsbury's that afternoon.

Like Curtis and many other women, I felt too much shame around my own sexuality to explore it through masturbation when I was growing up. And this was despite the fact that I grew up in a very liberal home, where my parents spoke about sex fairly openly. Of course, this is not the case for everyone, given that many conservative cultures actively discourage women from speaking openly about sex, particularly when they are young. That was the case for Poppy Jay, co-host of the BBC Asian Network's *Brown Girls Do It Too* podcast, who grew up in east London in a conservative Muslim home where sex was never mentioned; she's not even sure there's a word for it in Bengali. 'Masturbating felt so shameful growing up,' Jay told me. 'You immediately felt "dirty" after you had done the "deed". I was raised to believe any kind of self-care was *haram* [forbidden by Islamic law] as fuck and you were collecting hell Nectar points every time you pleasured yourself, especially if you were a woman.'

Masturbation felt equally shameful for Jay's co-host, Rubina Pabani, who also grew up in a Muslim home where sex was rarely discussed. She told me that being caught with her hands down her pants remains her 'biggest fear' to this day. 'When I was young I didn't even know what I was doing, it was like sneezing or satisfying an itch – masturbating was something my body needed to do. But we couldn't talk about it, it was something sneaky and dirty and if you enjoyed doing it then you were a slut. I was such a slut.'

It wasn't just that the act of masturbating itself felt wrong, but because neither Jay nor Pabani had anyone whom they felt comfortable talking with, they didn't know how to do it properly. 'I remember it being quite an isolating experience, fumbling around in the dark, sometimes literally and figuratively,' Jay said. 'I had no one to talk to, I couldn't even talk about wanking with my friends or cousins – it was 100 per cent a no-go area. Feeling pleasure and then being racked with guilt was a normalised experience for me . . . that is, until the internet was born.'

It's not novel to talk about female masturbation in 2021.

Look at how Phoebe Waller-Bridge's Fleabag proudly masturbated to a clip of Barack Obama delivering a speech in her cult TV show of the same name. Or how Michaela Coel wanked while pretending to be Beyoncé in her debut TV series, *Chewing Gum*. Then consider the long list of female celebrities who have sought to destigmatise masturbation by talking openly about it, from Emma Watson and Gwyneth Paltrow to Lena Dunham. Finally, we have got to a place where it no longer feels like women wanking has to be such a shameful act. But it's taken too long to get here, and the ramifications of growing up in a society that stigmatises female pleasure are still felt in relationships around the world.

Hence why we have something called The Orgasm Gap, a term used by University of Florida professor Laurie Mintz, author of *Becoming Cliterate: Why Orgasm Equality Matters – And How to Get It*. The Orgasm Gap refers to the fact that heterosexual women, on average, have fewer orgasms than heterosexual men. In her book, Mintz cites a 2016 study from the *Archives of Sexual Behavior* that looked at more than 52,500 American adults and which found that 95 per cent of straight men reported usually or always reaching orgasm during sex, compared to just 65 per cent of heterosexual women. The issue, Mintz argues, is that there is a cultural lack of understanding with regards to clitoral stimulation, which is necessary for most women to come. And yes, this ignorance is partly fuelled by porn because, as Gallop pointed out, we don't tend to see clitoral stimulation in mainstream porn, where women seem to come quicker than you can say 'orgasm'.

It's time to start prioritising female pleasure in the porn that most people are watching, i.e. the stuff you'll find on tube sites. Otherwise, women will wind up faking it and before you know it, that slug that slithered in your vagina will be slithering around someone else's.

Porn has a lot to answer for when it comes to body image. Take pubic hair, something that is often linked to porn due to the fact that the majority of female porn stars seem to be entirely hairless from the eyebrows down. But women have been shaving their body hair long before porn existed. In fact, they did so in Ancient Greece, when, according to Victoria Sherrow's book *Encyclopedia of Hair: A Cultural History*, a full bush was believed to be 'uncivilized'. Despite many noble attempts to combat this archaic view today – see copious adverts featuring women in swimwear with tufts of hair poking out at the sides and the annual #Januhairy campaign on social media – the majority of women still feel compelled to groom their pubic hair to some degree. Me included.

In 2017, a survey by *Cosmopolitan* found that only 6 per cent of women left their pubic hair au natural. The same survey also shed light on how much straight men care about their partner's pubic hair, with 30 per cent saying that it can be a relationship deal-breaker if the way it has been groomed doesn't suit their tastes. Another 40 per cent had even asked their partners to change the way they groom their pubic hair.* Of course, porn is not entirely to blame for this. But I find it hard to believe that it has nothing to do with it. Being hairless in conventional porn makes sense, partly because of the way that it glorifies youth, which is

---

* *Cosmopolitan* survey. Available at: https://www.cosmopolitan. com/sex-love/a9535211/pubic-hair-removal-trends-stats/

synonymous with a hairless vagina, and because it eliminates any obstacles to the clitoris – thus making everything nice and simple.

I've been getting rid of my pubic hair since I was 16. The first time was at a local beauty clinic near where I went to school in Somerset. I went with my best mate, both of us dosed up on paracetamol and primed for our Hollywood waxes, where you get everything taken off. I mean every last follicle. I'm not sure why we chose this type of wax as our first, given that it is the most painful and the most invasive. But it soon became a ritual, one I would adopt on a monthly basis for many years. I could lie and tell you I kept this up because I simply liked the way it made me feel – cleaner and sexier – but the truth is that I did it in case I went to a party and a boy put their hands down my pants.

As anyone who's ever tried it will attest, hair removal is no picnic. Pain aside, it's awkward and expensive, with research suggesting that women spend up to five figures a year on hair removal if they have treatments regularly.* There are several methods, each at different price points and with varying degrees of efficiency. Here are some of the most common ones.

- Shaving: Cheap, painless and effective, but it won't last for long, will give you stubble, and can cause your hair to grow back thicker and more determined.
- Epilating: If you have your own epilator then it's cheap, but feels as though someone's pricking a thousand

---

* A 2017 study by Centros Unico found that women who wax twice a month will spend around £23,000 on this activity during their lifetime.

needles into your body at once. Anyone who does this
on their pubic hair is a full-blown sadist.

- Waxing: Painful but over quickly, makes hair thinner but
  can cause ingrown hairs. A bit weird when you have to
  go on all fours and pry open your butt cheeks while a
  stranger lathers hot wax in your crevices.

- Laser-hair removal: Disgustingly expensive, long-lasting,
  only really works on people with dark hair. Also a bit
  weird when you have to go on all fours and pry open
  your butt cheeks while a stranger puts a hot beeping
  machine in your crevices.

I have dabbled in all of the above over the years. For a long
time, waxing was my thing. But after an ingrown hair led to
a cyst that led to me on a course of antibiotics, I soon switched
to laser hair removal, funding my first package of sessions at
the age of 21 by working in a juice shop for three weeks.
Little did I know that six years later, I'd still be forking over
a hefty portion of my salary to pay for it.

Let the record state that getting rid of your pubic hair
doesn't make you a bad feminist, just as wearing a T-shirt with
the word on it doesn't make you a good one. We spoke about
this on the podcast with sex educator Alix Fox. 'Pubic hair
has been made into such a feminist issue. And I am absolutely
a feminist. But I enjoy the feeling of removing some of my
pubic hair,' she said. Fox revealed how, at the time of recording,
hers was shaved into the shape of a fox's head. 'I am very on
brand,' she teased. We were talking about pubic hair in the
context of getting ready for your first date with someone. 'You
know how Olympic swimmers shave off all their body hair
before a big race? For me it's like getting in the zone and I

want to be streamlined and slick and I'm going to blow their mind by being an ice rink covered in baby oil.' I agree with Fox, there is something almost reassuring about prepping for a date in this way. It gets you in the mood, but it also boosts your confidence – or at least it boosts mine. But would we really feel like that, and subconsciously associate body confidence with a hairless vagina, if we, and the people we were shagging, didn't see it in porn?

Porn has long glorified a homogenised version of the female body, one that mirrors the same assets rewarded in Hollywood: youth, slimness and big breasts. A recent survey by *Cosmopolitan* found that these are the three main attributes men look for in a female porn star, presumably because that's what porn stars looked like in the porn they watched growing up. The only time you see plus-size women in conventional pornography is when they are being fetishised – something that is so popular in porn that it even has its own acronym: BBW (Big Beautiful Women). This all adds to the pressures women are under with regards to their appearance. Just like advertising campaigns, fashion magazines and films, porn perpetuates the myth that women need to squash themselves into smaller bodies in order to be deemed conventionally attractive. But porn stands out from other media as it can affect our body image in more intimate ways, too. Look at the rise of penis enlargement surgery, instances of which have been steadily increasing since the 1990s. This link has been blamed on porn due to the fact that male viewers compare themselves to the *very* well-endowed porn stars on screen, thus being made to feel inadequate as a result.

As for women, consider the rising 'designer vagina' trend that has spiked in recent years. The procedure can involve anything from reshaping vaginal lips to reducing the size of the labia or making it more symmetrical. In 2010, Harley Medical Group, a leading cosmetic surgery provider across the UK, reported receiving more than 5,000 enquiries for cosmetic gynaecology. More than half of these requests were for labial reduction, the rest for tightening and reshaping. Given that one of the only circumstances in which we see vaginas and penises up close outside of sex is in porn, it would be negligent not to make the links here.

Let's talk about the way that watching porn impacts sexual function. It's a contentious topic, one that is often hotly disputed among psychosexologists and sex educators. You've probably heard that men who watch porn are more likely to suffer from erectile dysfunction. But the reality is that the science has never been there to prove such a link. 'Porn itself is not damaging to people's sex lives or sexual function,' said Dr Karen Gurney, clinical psychologist at The Havelock Clinic and author of *Mind the Gap: The truth about desire and how to futureproof your sex life*. What is damaging, Dr Gurney told me, is when porn consumption is combined with poor sex education and/or a lack of healthy discussions around sex, which is the reality for a lot of millennials who, like me, did not grow up with adequate sex education. 'The problem comes when your reference for learning about sex comes from porn, as it does for many people,' Dr Gurney adds. 'It can then be difficult to not take what you've learned from porn and bring it into your sexual encounters. This can often cause problems, but the answer to this is better sex education and increasing the porn literacy of young people, not necessarily demonising porn itself.'

If porn isn't to blame for sexual dysfunction, what then? We spoke about this on the podcast with life coach and social media influencer Ben Bidwell, aka The Naked Professor. Bidwell has a condition known as delayed ejaculation, which is when a man finds it very difficult to ejaculate and rarely does. Delayed ejaculation, sometimes referred to as male orgasmic disorder, is not as common as issues such as erectile dysfunction and premature ejaculation – when a man ejaculates too quickly during intercourse – but its impact can be one of the more debilitating with regards to relationships. 'Some [women] take it very personally,' Bidwell said. 'I don't want who I'm with to be thinking that, so if it leads down the line where we're in a relationship and we're going to have sex at some point, I brief them. I say, "Look this is what shows up sometimes. I don't want us to think about it, it's not a big deal, I just don't want you to take it personally if it happens."' Bidwell said that he still enjoys sex but that it's pleasurable 'in a different way', adding: 'I obviously don't get as much enjoyment out of it as other men and women.'

While there are physical causes to sexual dysfunction, such as certain cancers or organ issues, it is usually a psychological issue. This was the case for Bidwell, who spent years trying to find physiological ways to overcome his condition to no avail. He started looking for psychological causes by attending counselling, but that didn't help either. 'I believe this is here to teach me, because through my twenties, I wasn't showing who really I was,' Bidwell explained. 'I wasn't embracing my emotions, I was just living in a bit of a sort of society's box.' Now, however, he feels that living with the condition has allowed him to become more authentic and emotionally open. 'All these things I wasn't. So, I've become all those things and [the delayed ejaculation] is the final hurdle. But I feel like I'm almost ready to let it go. I feel mentally ready to let it go.'

We didn't discuss whether or not porn had impacted Bidwell's condition, or his understanding of it, in the episode. I sent him a message on Instagram to ask. 'I stopped connecting with porn for a long time,' he replied, via voice note. When he was younger, Bidwell explained he would look at images of naked women in magazines. 'And you know, I'd find it exciting, just the odd photo. Then the internet came along and suddenly images weren't enough, it was videos. And then I needed more and more and more.' It got to a point where he would scroll for hours through various videos, looking for something to take his fancy. But nothing did. 'I knew it wasn't healthy,' he added. 'I used to be so excited by just a glimpse and then that wasn't sufficient.' He sought the help of a psychosexologist, who helped him find a healthier balance with the way he was consuming porn, which, looking back, he realises had in fact 'numbed [his] senses, a bit'. The science behind this is conflicting, but one study from 2014 found that men who watch a lot of porn tend to have less grey matter and reactivity in the part of the brain related to our reward system. The researchers estimated that this could mean one of two things: either that watching porn shrinks this pleasure-related region in the brain, or that having this brain configuration makes it more enjoyable to watch porn, and so people with this configuration will simply be more inclined to watch porn more often.

One of the most troubling things about porn is the fetishisation of ethnic minorities. The most-searched term on Pornhub in 2019 was 'Japanese' followed by 'Hentai' (pornography containing anime and manga). 'Korean' was in fifth place, while 'Chinese' was eighteenth. The fetishisation of Asian women in porn is so rife that it has almost become socially acceptable to make light of it. Consider Amy Schumer's 'bit' from her 2012 show *Mostly Sex Stuff*, in which she told a rapturous audience: 'It doesn't matter what you do, ladies, every guy is going to leave you for an Asian woman. They're smarter. They laugh like this [Schumer puts her hand over her mouth] because they know that men hate when women speak. Oh, and how do they bring it home for the win? The smallest vaginas in the game.' In a piece for *Refinery29*, sex worker Lily Yin called Schumer's comments 'tone-deaf, particularly for a woman who's made a career out of highlighting everyday sexism' and pointed out how unnervingly comfortable Schumer seemed when making such an offensive statement.* 'Asian women are constantly sexualized and objectified by society,' she wrote, explaining how she benefited from her race in the sex industry. 'My Asian heritage has been a very lucrative selling point. When I worked at an all-Asian dungeon, there was never a single day that we didn't have an influx of clients coming to see us, preferring a dominant Asian woman to any other type of dominatrix.'

It's not just Asian women that are fetishised, either. Pornhub's list of the most-searched terms also included words such as 'ebony', 'Latina' and 'Indian'. Meanwhile, in a report titled *Racism in Pornography*, authors Alice Mayall and Diana

---

* 'How It Feels To Be Fetishised As An Asian Sex Worker', Lily Yin, June 2016. Available at: https://www.refinery29.com/en-gb/2016/06/112654/asian-women-fetish-sex-stereotype

E.H. Russell provided examples of racist porn film titles including, 'Animal Sex Among Black Women', 'Geisha's Girls', and 'Gang Banged by Blacks'.*

The way that pornography fetishises ethnic minorities is 'textbook racism', said Sangeeta Pillai, founder of the Soul Sutras platform, which tackles taboos surrounding South Asian women and sexuality. 'We become a tick box on a website. It's so easy to lump a certain type of person into a category, without thinking about the multitudes that even people of a single race carry within themselves.'

Pillai told me she has experienced fetishisation in her own love life, with men asking her if she does the Kama Sutra. 'Like the Kama Sutra was some sort of thing that every Indian woman learns in her cradle.' She added that these comments were usually from educated, liberal men. 'They clearly couldn't be bothered to educate themselves about my culture. And I'm guessing a lot of their "Kama Sutra" comments perhaps came from porn, which isn't known for complex cultural depictions.'

The fact that hardcore pornography capitalises on racist stereotypes is something porn performers are aware of, too. The adult actor Asa Akira has previously said that her Japanese heritage 'guarantees' her work, while former performer Vanessa Belmond has said that she and her boyfriend left the sex industry after they were both constantly asked to play up to stereotypes based on their ethnicities. 'My boyfriend grew to hate doing porn, because he was constantly told to act more like a thug stereotype,' she said. 'He got passed up many times because he was not dark enough, and because he was uncom-

---

* Available at: http://pornharmsresearch.com/wp-content/uploads /2012/03/24163417-Racism-in-Pornography.pdf

fortable being rough with women and calling them racist names. He wasn't good at playing into the "scary black man" persona, so directors went for the guys that could.'

There is little research into the impact of racial fetishisation and stereotyping in porn. But one study from 2018 as published in the *Archives of Sexual Behaviour* found that out of 172 free porn videos found online, content featuring black, Latino and Asian men was more likely to depict male aggression compared to that which featured white men. Similarly, videos featuring Asian and Latina women were more likely to depict them as suffering at the hands of aggressive male co-stars.

Sociologist and critical race feminist, Golshan Golriz, who co-authored the study, told me the impacts of racial fetishisation in porn are far-reaching, but the most urgent one is its presentation of sexual violence against ethnic minorities. 'Racial fetishisation can have grave consequences for women vis-a-vis sexual assault and sexual harassment, both institutionally and in everyday life. It can also contribute to the violent and deadly criminalization of men of colour, who are often portrayed as being sexually aggressive,' she said. As for how we overcome this, Golriz explained it's not even a question that can be answered at this stage given that the consequences of this kind of representation have yet to be thoroughly understood from a psychological perspective. 'But I can certainly say that systematic analysis provides a useful starting point for understanding how representation may impact crises such as violence against women.'

Whether or not porn leads to more real-life sexual violence is a hotly disputed topic; one that rears its head every time a sex criminal is found to be an avid porn viewer. Some research has found links between the two. For example, a report from the World Health Organization linked sexual violence and the proliferation of coercive sexual fantasies to access to porn. Meanwhile, a recent government-led report found some trends between access to porn and sexual harassment that calls for further research, stating: 'People who find legal pornography acceptable are generally more likely to find sexual harassment acceptable than people who find legal pornography unaccept-able.' The government report also highlighted links between the consumption of porn and sexist attitudes, which could then lead to sexually aggressive behaviours.* However, there is also a lot of research that heavily disputes making links between porn and sexual violence, with one recent study stating that 'it is time to discard the hypothesis that pornography contributes to increased sexual assault behavior'.†

One researcher, Neil Malamuth at the University of California, Los Angeles, who has carried out many studies exploring the link between porn and sexual violence, concluded that porn was a bit like alcohol, explaining that on its own, it may pose no threat. But for some people with other risk factors, it could lead to dangerous behaviours. But ultimately, further research was needed to prove either point.

What is clear, though, is that porn contains a lot of sexual violence. And I mean, loads. One study from 2010 found that out of 304 porn scenes analysed, 88.2 per cent contained phys-ical aggression, spanking, gagging and slapping. 'Perpetrators of aggression were usually male, whereas targets of aggression

---

* Available at: https://publications.parliament.uk/pa/cm201719/cmselect/cmwomeq/701/70107.htm#footnote-104
† Available at: https://www.sciencedirect.com/science/article/abs/pii/S1359178909000445

were overwhelmingly female,' the study states, adding that 'targets most often showed pleasure or responded neutrally to the aggression'.* That's the most concerning bit, isn't it? It's one thing watching violence against women on screen, but when the woman appears to be deriving pleasure from that violence, that's the kind of thing that teaches women like me to moan when their male partner grabs their neck a bit too hard during sex instead of saying it really fucking hurts. It's the kind of thing that tells men that this is what all women like. And if they look like they're in pain, that just means they're enjoying themselves.

We spoke about the links between porn and violence on one of our first episodes of the podcast with sex writer and influencer Hannah Witton, whose comments echoed those of Malamuth and Dr Gurney. 'The thing that makes [porn] dangerous is the lack of sex education,' she said. 'We're never going to get rid of porn. It's the internet. You can't regulate it and censor it. That's an impossible task. But what we can do is educate people.' She argued that while you might see violent and non-consensual scenarios on screen, because ultimately we cannot control pornographic content, what you can do is educate people to the degree that they can view that kind of porn and not be interested in it because they can recognise it as harmful.

When I spoke to Cindy Gallop with regards to the links between sexual violence in porn, she had a very unique point of view. 'Everything that worries people about porn is entirely due to business issues,' she told me over the phone from her

---

* Available at: https://journals.sagepub.com/doi/abs/10.1177/1077801210382866

very plush-looking New York residence. 'Porn has fallen prey to the business theory I call "collaborative competition". That's when everybody in a sector competes with everyone else in a sector by doing exactly what everybody else in the sector is doing.' This is why Gallop believes the rise of violence in porn is not due to 'evil' people in the industry nor to people having become depraved human beings wanting to watch violent content, but due to 'a bunch of guys, scared shitless because the porn industry is tanking as so much of it is free, and so they're not making any money, and they're playing it safe'. Unfortunately, playing it safe means conforming to the most damaging types of porn aimed at the male gaze.

In light of all this, it would be really easy to turn around and say, 'all porn is awful and violent and we should ban it completely'. There are a lot of anti-porn activists who say just that and have long campaigned for the abolition of porn. Like Julia Long, who, in her book, *Anti-Porn: The Resurgence of Anti-Pornography Feminism*, blames porn for many societal issues, ranging from the objectification of the female body and violence against women to the wider 'pornification' of Western society. For Long, being against porn is integral to her feminism. This used to be the case for author and comedian Sara Pascoe, until she started researching porn for her first book, *Animal: The Autobiography of a Female Body*. 'I realised everything I knew about porn had come via feminism and what that meant was that it had a very strong agenda that wasn't necessarily correct in a lot of ways,' she said when she came on the podcast to discuss her second book, *Sex Power Money*. 'I would have probably argued that the fact that porn exists makes straight men see women as sexually available all the time.' Pascoe explained that her view of porn was also shaped by the straight men she knew who had developed pornography addictions. 'I assumed all straight men were existing at maybe a slightly lower level, that they couldn't help walk into shops and imagine women naked and walking down the street and having sex with everyone,' she said. While porn addictions are a very real and very dangerous thing, the reality is that a lot of people have a fairly healthy relationship with porn. 'It's a release, it's fantasy, they know it's not real, it can be either different or separate from what they do with their partners, but that's not as interesting,' Pascoe added. It may also help you identify what you might like in bed, which would have been very useful for me when Mr Slug asked me that exact question. There's even an increasing body of research that suggests watching porn as a couple can be beneficial to your relationship.*

The core issue with all this is not porn. It goes back to something I said at the start of this chapter, which is that when we talk about porn, we tend to talk about just one type. If you branch away from the mainstream porn that dominates the tube sites, what you'll find is a whole range of adult content online that is both realistic *and* empowering. There are so many changemakers in the adult industry who are making films that combat all the issues I've mentioned here, from the lack of physical and sexual diversity to racial fetishisation and violence against women. The difference is that you have to pay for it.

Gallop is one of these changemakers. Her company, Make Love Not Porn, is the world's first user-generated, human

---

* Available at: https://www.ncbi.nlm.nih.gov/pmc/articles/PMC6155976/

curated, social sex video sharing platform. 'We are a counterpoint to porn, if porn is the Hollywood movie, we are the real-world documentary,' Gallop told me, describing her platform as sparking a 'social sex revolution'. What Make Love Not Porn does is allow regular people to upload regular videos of themselves having sex. These then go through a series of curators, who will check to see if they meet a certain set of standards before being uploaded to the website, sort of like YouTube, but with sex. 'We are socialising and normalising sex in order to make it easier for everyone to talk about it and to promote consent, good sexual behaviours and good sexual values,' said Gallop. 'We celebrate real world bodies, real world hair, real world penis size, breast size. You can talk body positivity all you like, but nothing makes you feel great about your own body like watching people who are nobody's aspirational body types getting turned on by each other. Porn teaches you that sex is a performance, this is doing the opposite.'

I have no doubt that we would feel more comfortable in our own bodies if we could see them being desired on-screen, particularly in a way that was respectful and consensual. The tragedy, though, is that projects like Gallop's are unlikely to gain much traction in today's society, one that still views sex and porn as taboo.

Despite the fact that what Gallop is doing is quite clearly helpful and important, many people refuse to work with her to help build her platform. 'They view us under the umbrella of "adult content",' she said, explaining how major companies such as PayPal, American Express and MailChimp have an all-out ban on adult content. 'No one will associate [with] what they think is pornography. I have to go to people at the top of the company, explain what I'm doing and beg to use their services,' she said. 'Every single payment processor that will not process payments for legal adult companies, every single bank that will not bank a legal adult venture, every single business that will not partner with an adult content company, they are responsible for all the bad things that happen in the adult industry,' Gallop concluded. 'When you force an entire industry underground, you make it very difficult for good things to happen, and a whole lot easier for bad things to happen.'

Another person pushing for change in the adult industry is the Swedish filmmaker Erika Lust, who is frequently referred to as one of the figureheads in the feminist porn movement. Unlike conventional porn, Lust's films celebrate consent and female pleasure, and she casts people of all body shapes, sizes and physical abilities. 'I want to show and capture the whole feeling of sex,' she told me over e-mail. Unlike in conventional porn films, where plots are rendered obsolete, for Lust, they are everything, as is character development. 'When we think about porn, we think about the films you can find over the free tube sites; adult movies mainly made by white cisgender men, where you have close up genital shots and emotionless storylines. With my films, I want to portray healthy sex relationships on screen in which consent is shown clearly and both women and men are in charge of what they do with their bodies whether the film is romantic, kinky, or anything in between.'

Lust is also a keen advocate of safe sets and protecting her performers, something that is severely lacking in the amateur porn sector – watch Rashida Jones' *Hot Girls Wanted* documentary to see how horrifically unethical and exploitative some adult filmmakers can be. Lust doesn't typecast performers based on their age, race, sexuality, or gender and, when shooting films, she is careful not to direct them too intimately and speaks to each of them ahead of time to get a sense of what they are and are not comfortable with. 'I allow them to have sex that feels organic and natural to them. I want performers to be focused on each other instead of posing for the camera.'

Like Gallop, Lust is a keen advocate of promoting positive conversations around porn, which is why she launched the non-profit website, ThePornConversation.Org, to encourage parents to speak to their children about adult content. 'We can't stop children from finding porn online, so it's really important to give them the tools to be critical and aware of what they're watching. They should be able to understand the difference between the types of porn and what sex between consenting adults is,' she said.

Another adult filmmaker making waves in the feminist porn scene is Jennifer Lyon Bell, whose production company Blue Artichoke Films produces a range of award-winning adult films that champion intimacy and communication in sex. 'Communication during sex is super hot,' Bell told me. 'It shows that you're willing to take a risk and be vulnerable with the other person, because, let's be honest, sometimes you have to be a little brave to ask for things just the way you want them. In my new film, *Wild Card*, the two performers are given a game to play with each other, and they absolutely have to communicate and engage with each other in order to succeed in the game and get what they want sexually. It's so charming and sexy to watch them become more and more comfortable in asking for what they want.'

There's also an emerging group of queer and non-binary

adult filmmakers who are fighting against the lack of healthy LGBT+ sex scenes that celebrate rather than fetishise sexual minorities. Take Shine Louise Houston, who was working in a sex shop when she noticed the distinct lack of queer porn on offer, and decided to take matters into her own hands. In her first film, *Crash Pad* (2006), she cast Jiz Lee, a non-binary artist and porn novice. She soon launched her own company, Pink and White productions, which dubs itself the 'hot bed of queer sexual cinema'.

There is so much positive change happening in the porn world. But in order to really make a tangible difference to the way that adult content is consumed, we have to change not just the content but the way we talk about it. The films that Lust, Houston and Bell make are all brilliant (and *very* hot), but they are behind a paywall. They are also not hugely well-known to those outside of the adult industry, at least not when you compare their content to what is available on Pornhub and the other tube sites. Paying for porn needs to become the norm, but so does talking about it. Because had I grown up with even a semblance of the knowledge of porn that I have now, I know that it wouldn't have impacted my sexual experiences in the way that it has. As Gallop and Witton said, the problem is not with porn, it's with the lack of conversations and education around everything to do with sex, from masturbation and pubic hair to female pleasure and the orgasm gap. So, let's talk. Only then can we begin to bring porn out of the shadows and start having better sex.

Chapter Eight
Hunting Witches

On 5 October 2017, the world changed. After decades of furious whispers, failed investigations and countless non-disclosure agreements, Harvey Weinstein, one of Hollywood's most powerful producers, was exposed as a serial rapist. Overnight, the man renowned for producing films such as *Pulp Fiction* and *Good Will Hunting* became a symbol for how unbridled power facilitates unbridled evil. The kind of evil that exploits vulnerability, ruins careers and in some cases, drives people to suicide. And yet, it took almost forty years – the first alleged assault happened in 1980 – to hold him to account. As more allegations against Weinstein and other powerful men emerged, people became increasingly devastated, furious and appalled. But they were also galvanised.

The #MeToo movement was founded in 2006 by the American activist and sexual assault survivor Tarana Burke, who began using the phrase as a way of supporting fellow women of colour who had experienced sexual violence. But the movement went viral in the wake of the Weinstein allegations, when the actress Alyssa Milano called on women who had been sexually harassed or assaulted to tweet the words 'Me Too' to 'give people a sense of the magnitude of the problem'. It was an invitation many had waited their whole lives for. I don't need to tell you what happened next.

As the hundreds and thousands of stories of abuse, assault and harassment flooded the internet, I read them in shock. Many of the allegations were, like those against Weinstein, within a working environment. But just as many were within a romantic one, too, where the lines between what is and is not consensual can look blurrier, despite the fact that there's absolutely nothing blurry about sexual assault. I watched from the side-lines as celebrities, activists and actors chimed in with their own harrowing experiences. Some involved rape, others attempted rape. Some reported their experiences, but most did not. Before #MeToo, the word 'rape' was one I associated with strange men dragging young, screaming women into dark alleys. That narrative was so entrenched in me that when I read #MeToo stories, I didn't see myself in any of them. I was one of the lucky ones, I thought. No one had ever touched me inappropriately or done anything to me without my consent. I'd never been sexually assaulted, and neither had any of my friends. How lucky we all were. It took two years for me to realise that none of this was true.

I remember the night quite clearly. June 2019. A pub in Shepherd's Bush. Five portions of fish and chips. My friend, let's call her Rosie, brought up #MeToo. She'd been thinking about it a lot recently, and how it made her rethink the night she was raped. This was news to us. We sat and listened in silence as Rosie recalled a party from when we were 16 – a party I had also been at. She was very drunk and passed out in our friend's bed. A few hours later, she woke up and found his body pressing on hers, his penis inside her. *I was in the bedroom next door*. We asked the obvious questions. Had she reported it? No. Had she sought therapy? Yes. Did it help? Sort of. Slowly, as we processed what had happened to Rosie, each and every one of us at that table started to open up about our own #MeToo stories – we all had one, but most of us had more than that.

Even after #MeToo, sexual violence remains widely misunderstood. A report by the End Violence Against Women (EVAW) coalition from December 2018 found that one-third of men thought that if before forcing non-consensual sex on a woman, she had flirted on a date, it generally wouldn't count as rape. One-fifth of women believed the same. Meanwhile, the same number of men said that a woman can't change her mind about consent after sex has started. A third of all those surveyed said they didn't think it was rape if a woman is pressured into having sex but there is no physical violence. And almost a quarter didn't think that, in most cases, sex without consent in long-term relationships is rape, despite the fact that laws against rape in marriage have been in place since 1991.

Here are a few facts about rape in England and Wales.*

- Twenty per cent of women and 4 per cent of men have experienced some type of sexual assault since the age of 16, equivalent to 3.4 million female and 631,000 male victims.
- Only around 15 per cent of those who experience sexual violence report it to the police.

---

* These stats were sourced from the charity Rape Crisis.

- Approximately 90 per cent of those who are raped know the perpetrator prior to the offence.
- Of young women aged 18–24, 31 per cent report having experienced sexual abuse in childhood.
- Most women in the UK do not have access to a Rape Crisis Centre.
- A third of people believe women who flirt are partially responsible for being raped.
- Conviction rates for rape are far lower than for other crimes, with only 5.7 per cent of reported rape cases ending in a conviction for the perpetrator.

The stories shared by me and my friends all subscribe to the above stats. None of our experiences included physical violence. None of us reported them. And we all knew our perpetrators. In most cases, they were our friends.

I'd fancied Ben since I was 14. So, when, aged 18, I found myself snuggled next to him on a sofa after a party, I was thrilled. We'd flirted all evening; he could kiss me now. But he didn't. Instead, Ben pulled my body into his while we were lying on the sofa, lifting a blanket over us so the other fifteen sleeping bodies in the room couldn't see what he was about to do. When his hand slid into my underwear, I yelped in shock. No one had done that to me before. I didn't like it, so I tried to move his hand away. He put it back. I tried again, the hand returned. This back and forth persisted for several minutes. He whispered: 'Come on, I've fancied you for ages too.' I closed my eyes and tried to think of something else while he continued, slowly pushing his fingers inside me. It started to really hurt. I told him I felt sick and when Ben finally retracted his hand, I ran to the toilet and vomited. It was late at this point, and I was worried Ben would come looking for me. I locked the bathroom door, curled up on my friend's fluffy bathroom rug and went to sleep. The next morning, he acted as if nothing had happened.

I didn't register that night as an assault. Instead, I wrote it off as a bad sexual encounter that was down to my own lack of experience. It was my fault. I'd led him on, I was naive. I was *frigid*. The whole thing felt humiliating, so I buried it. Just like I buried it when, later that summer, another boy did the same thing. And then again when I went on holiday with a group of friends in Ibiza and, after passing out in a hotel room, woke up to find that one of the boys I'd gone away with had taken a photograph while I'd been sleeping of his testicles resting on my face.

It was only at that pub in Shepherd's Bush that I started to remember these experiences. When I shared them, I was half expecting my friends to laugh them off as the boys had done when I asked why they took that fucking photo. But they didn't. They used words like 'assault' and 'molestation', words I'd never attached to those memories. I'm not sure I'd even feel comfortable using them now.

Denial is incredibly common among people who have experienced sexual violence. There are many reasons for this. We live in a victim-blaming culture in which rape survivors are frequently gaslit and asked questioned such as: 'Did you leave your drink unattended?', 'What were you wearing?' and 'Had you taken drugs?'. As if answers to such questions could vindicate a rapist, which sadly they often do in court, where it's remarkably rare for sexual assault cases to end in convictions. For example, a rape trial in the Republic of Ireland in 2018 famously saw the defence lawyer use the fact that the woman was wearing a thong as 'evidence' of consent. 'You have to look at the way she was dressed,' the defence lawyer told the jury. 'She was wearing a thong with a lace front.' The 27-year-old man, accused of raping a 17-year-old girl, was found not guilty of rape shortly afterwards. Sadly, the view that sexual assault survivors only have themselves to blame is held by many women, too. Such as by Donna Rotunno, Harvey Weinstein's defence lawyer, who famously told a *New York Times* interviewer that she had never been raped because she 'would never put [herself] in that position'.

Then there's the belief that false reports of rape are common – they aren't – and the way sexual violence has been handled so clumsily in popular culture. It's either used to add drama (*Game of Thrones*), to invite audiences to question the credibility of rape survivors (*Liar*), to further the characterisation of male characters (also *Game of Thrones*), or it's twinned with suicide (*13 Reasons Why*). It took until 2020 for there to finally be an on-screen depiction of rape that resonated with survivors, courtesy of Michaela Coel's *I May Destroy You*, whose own assault inspired the storyline. The programme was lauded as an examination on consent and the multiple ways it is and is not given. Like when you have consensual sex with someone only for them to assault you almost immediately afterwards. Or when you have sex with someone only to later find out that they lied to you about their sexuality. Or when you have a threesome with two strangers, and then realise they might have known each other before. None of those encounters are completely consensual. And while that might be obvious to the person experiencing it, it isn't always to others.

With all that in mind, then, perhaps it's no surprise that myself and my friends repressed our #MeToo stories for years.

We hadn't been taught to recognise them as assault. We had been conditioned to brush them off and blame ourselves. And we are not the only people who have done this, of course. I put a call out on social media asking for stories from people who, like us, had recently reflected on their previous sexual encounters and realised that many of them were not entirely consensual. Here are some of their stories.

I had one conversation with girlfriends where we discussed #MeToo stories that had happened to us. I told them the story of how I lost my virginity and one of my girlfriends said 'well that's rape'. I hadn't ever viewed it that way before. She was right, and I knew that, but I had never felt I could claim that before. Because it wasn't violent and with some stranger in a dark alley, I didn't feel I could claim that word as mine. It didn't feel 'big' enough of an experience. Prior to #MeToo, I thought non-consensual sex was violent, an attack, 'obvious'. Hearing other stories made me realise it can be a lot more subtle and that it was something that I had indeed experienced.

My first sexual experience that I felt I hadn't consented to was with a guy that I had known for a little while and had slept with previously. I had gone back to his after a night out with friends and we had had fun, fully consensual sex, just like we had done previously. I fell asleep naked on my front. I woke in the middle of the night to him on top of me attempting to insert himself into me. I had just woken up, so was dazed anyway but once I realised what was happening I completely froze. I knew I wanted him to stop but I couldn't speak so I just lay there. He was having trouble inserting himself so after a short while I told him to stop, that I was too sleepy to have sex but he persisted with 'it's okay babe'. I rolled over onto my back and he had sex with me. In the morning I felt sick to my stomach. We'd had such great sex before, but I couldn't get my head around the fact that he would want to have sex with me whilst I was clearly asleep, practically unconscious. It made me feel that there was no respect for me as a person and that I was there in his bed purely for the purpose of having sex. I felt weak for letting him have sex with me after I had said 'no' but it seemed easier to just let him get on with it. I decided against telling friends what had happened because I knew they would have said that I should have been more forceful with my 'no', but at the time it just didn't seem that easy.

When I was 15 years old, I decided I wanted to drink with my friends. A boy from my school was having a bonfire that me and two other girls decided to attend together. When we arrived at the bonfire, there were five boys there, one of whom was called Joseph. We began to drink, and Joseph kept pushing me to drink more, handing me a beer and saying 'chug with me'. He kept apologising to one of the girls I came to the party with for 'what he did last time', which at the time didn't make sense to me, (until later in the night when we got home and she explained that he's super 'touchy' and 'weird' with drunk girls). Joseph tried to encourage everybody to strip and go into the pool, which they did. One of the boys at the party made me stay back because I was obviously too drunk, which I am thankful for. When everybody got back, I noticed Joseph kept trying to 'help' me. The boys at the party kept telling him to stay away from me, which confused me more than anything. He was being clingy, but wasn't that what drunk people did? I went to lay down, and Joseph was following me. Immediately the boys yelled at him again, telling him to leave me alone and let me sleep. Reluctantly, he went away, saying 'dude I just wanna help her'. I was again confused, but too drunk and tired to care. I fell asleep. I'm not sure how much time had passed when I woke up, but immediately I noticed Joseph lying next to me. His hand was on my vagina. Nobody realised what was going on because there was a blanket on top of me. I got up. I'm not sure to what extent he touched me. It's been four years. It took me a year to fully process the fact that I had been molested, and even longer for me to speak out in fear that, because it took me so long to process what happened, nobody would believe me. When I left the party that night, I felt like a slut. I had a boyfriend at the time and even though I knew I never consented to Joseph touching me, I felt like I had somehow cheated on him. I knew what had happened was wrong, but I didn't think it was 'serious' enough for it to be sexual assault, so in turn, I blamed myself. So many victims are unable to recognise what has happened to them as sexual assault or rape until much later. Trauma is processed differently by everybody, and nobody's experience should be invalidated by this.

The scary thing is that quite a few of my sexual experiences haven't been consensual. A guy I was seeing and really liked, pressured me to have sex in the shower. When I said I didn't want to and got out and laid on the bed — he came up behind me and forced himself inside of me. I froze. You don't always say or do anything when you're in shock but people *who haven't been in that position sometimes question you if you haven't. I had another boyfriend who forced himself on me twice in our relationship when he was drunk. He was abusive and controlling and would constantly talk about raping me. Unlike the other incident, I reported this when I got out of the relationship, but the police challenged me on why I didn't report it at the time and told me domestic rapes don't tend to go to court as there's often no forensics, witnesses, or CCTV. I also had the father of my ex stroke my vagina once on the outside of my clothes when I was upset about something and asked for a hug. Again, I just froze. It's frightening to think how many men get away with sexual assault because women fear they won't be believed if they report it. The system is dangerously flawed.*

When the musician and actor Jordan Stephens joined me on the podcast, he was very open about how #MeToo forced him to re-examine the way he'd behaved with women in the past. 'I was very good at pointing fingers,' the Rizzle Kicks singer said. 'I hadn't necessarily looked at my own patterns.' As I said in Chapter One, Stephens explained that while he had never physically abused anyone, he recognised 'a parallel on a smaller scale', citing coercive control and emotional neglect. 'I haven't been to the more extreme end,' he added. 'I do feel as though the energy behind that, or let's say the suppressed pain or wounds that manifest that kind of behaviour, I definitely have my own version of that. My actions as a result of that wound have I think been something I've wanted to change.'

What struck me about Stephens' comments was that while he owned up to his own mistakes, he immediately separated himself from those at 'the more extreme end', e.g. the Weinsteins of the world. I understand why he did that – but by explicitly making that distinction, Stephens highlighted one of the core controversies of the #MeToo movement: that there is a spectrum of sexual violence, one that can belittle certain experiences and dramatise others.

And so that brings me back to Weinstein. I was gripped by the media coverage of the allegations against him. Not just because of the sheer volume of claims against him and how far back they stretched, but because I was shocked at how long it took for them to make it to print. It's now well-known that many people in the film industry had heard rumours of Weinstein's misconduct – if not about the allegations of assault and harassment, then at least about how he bullied and humiliated his staff. And yet, all this was accepted for years. So much so that Weinstein's abhorrent behaviour was frequently used as a punchline in jokes. Like in 2005, when Courtney Love was asked on a red carpet if she had any advice for aspiring female actors: 'I'll get libeled if I say it,' she replied, smirking, before adding: 'If Harvey Weinstein invites you to a private party in the Four Seasons, don't go.' The reporter laughed.

Then, there was the moment when Seth MacFarlane presented the Oscar for the best supporting actress category in 2013, during which he told the nominees: 'Congratulations, you five ladies no longer have to pretend to be attracted to Harvey Weinstein.' Again, the audience erupted into laughter. It was only after #MeToo that the comedian clarified that his joke was his way of standing up to Weinstein after his friend, the actress Jessica Barth, had confided in him about her 2011 experience with the producer. As reported by Ronan

Farrow's *New Yorker* article, Weinstein allegedly invited Barth up to his hotel room for a meeting, only for her to find champagne and sushi. She claimed that the producer requested she give him a naked massage. The fact that MacFarlane knew that story and felt confident enough to make a joke about Weinstein facing no repercussions for his alleged actions, proves just how entrenched his culture of abuse had become.

So, yes: Weinstein is an extreme case. It wasn't just that he'd allegedly sexually assaulted so many women. He was once the most powerful man in Hollywood. Some of the women who made allegations against him were movie stars – Gwyneth Paltrow, Cara Delevingne, Angelina Jolie – and the settlements his lawyers used to silence his accusers involved six-figure sums. After the Weinstein story broke, a series of other similarly 'extreme' cases followed. Such as the one against NBC news anchor Matt Lauer, who was accused of sexual harassment and assault by several of his female colleagues. And the US comedian Louis CK, who was accused of sexual misconduct by five women who outlined their claims in a *New York Times* article one month after the Weinstein allegations emerged. And then there was Kevin Spacey, who was accused of making sexual advances towards the actor Anthony Rapp when he was 14 and Spacey was 26. Many, many more cases followed, and by October 2018, *The New York Times* had published a list of 201 'powerful men' who had been brought down by #MeToo. They included CEOs, state senators, producers, directors . . . it was a reckoning.

While millions of sexual assault survivors were sharing their stories on social media, the ones that made headlines were the high profile cases. Which meant that, unless you went trawling through the replies to Alyssa Milano's tweet, the majority of the #MeToo stories you read would have been those that were 'on the extreme end'. But that's a problem, one that removes complexity from discussions around sexual assault.

When I interviewed Weinstein survivor Rowena Chiu for the *Independent*, she said that the problem with how we talk about #MeToo cases now is that 'there's a tendency to villainise the perpetrator'. 'We hear of these evil powerful men that hold young beautiful women down to beds. It's almost like a Disney story, where you have a hero and a villain. Because we don't talk about how someone like Harvey was very charming, or that everyone in Hollywood wanted to work for him. There's no room for nuance. So these predators become larger than life, which means people ignore the more prevalent peril of ordinary men and women who are abusing people within their remits. It's Joe in the corporate boardroom who puts his hand up a colleague's skirt, or Martin who makes an inappropriate comment in a meeting. That is all part of predation and harassment. But I'm telling you, these perpetrators think, "I'm no Harvey Weinstein, I'm no Roger Ailes, I'm no Bill Cosby, and therefore the #MeToo movement doesn't apply to me."'

If we subscribe to the way of thinking that Chiu describes, it vindicates abusers. Abusers who might have assaulted or harassed women but don't view themselves as predators because the stories surrounding Weinstein and others feel so far removed from their own, that they couldn't possibly see themselves as part of the problem. But the issue goes deeper than this, too. Because this way of thinking also encourages victims not to see themselves as victims. People like me and my friends look at the women who spoke up about Weinstein, Chiu included, and we hear stories involving champagne, film premieres and major Hollywood producers. We hear these stories and we think, 'Oh, well what happened to me was nowhere near as bad as that'. And so we push our own #MeToo stories further into the darkest corners of our mind until we forget they even happened. As I said, it took two years for me to realise that my experiences were a part of the #MeToo conversation. Because when the movement started, I didn't think I had the right to put my hand up and say: 'Me Too'.

It's important to recognise that it is a privilege to say 'me too'. Over the years, the movement has been criticised for being dominated by white female voices. One article that ran in December 2018 in *Medium* by Thalia Charles reminded readers that Burke's #MeToo began as a way of supporting women of colour who had survived sexual assault. 'Her Me Too was an effort to let those young women of color, often low-income and from fractured communities, know not only that they were not to blame for their victimhood but also they were not alone,' Charles wrote. She went on to point out that many of the loudest voices in the #MeToo movement were white cisgendered women. She named Milano alongside Weinstein survivors Rose McGowan, Asia Argento and Ashley Judd, whose #MeToo stories dominated news headlines for a period of time. This is why people, including Charles, argued that #MeToo 'perpetuated the idea of white female victimhood'. As Charles put it: 'When young women of colour say that they have been raped or sexually assaulted, they are not met with praise. Instead, derision, doubt and even more physical or psychological attacks shun them into silence, and who will speak for them? The white feminists who push WOC to the side of the movement founded for them?' The future success of #MeToo, she concluded, 'will be measured by how willing people are to widen their definitions and perspectives'.

You only need to look at the statistics with regards to sexual violence to see how necessary it is to widen the lens through which #MeToo is viewed. Sexual violence has a disproportionate impact on women of colour, disabled women and LGBT+ people. According to the National Center on Violence Against Women in the Black Community, one in five black women are survivors of rape and 35 per cent of black women experience some form of contact sexual violence during their lifetime. Meanwhile, the 2015 U.S. Transgender Survey found that 47 per cent of transgender people are sexually assaulted at some point in their lifetime, and 44 per cent of lesbians and 61 per cent of bisexual women experience rape, physical violence, or stalking by an intimate partner, compared to 35 per cent of straight women. Among people of colour, American Indian (65 per cent), multiracial (59 per cent), Middle Eastern (58 per cent) and black (53 per cent) respondents of the 2015 U.S. Transgender Survey were most likely to have been sexually assaulted in their lifetime.

It's crucial to bear this in mind when we talk about #MeToo, because it is so much easier for some people – women like me – to speak out than others. It is because of this, I suspect, that there are so many survivors whose stories we will never hear, Weinstein victims included. As Chiu told me in our interview: 'The Harvey survivors we know about are the tip of the iceberg. I know several who aren't public and probably never will be.'

It did not take long for the #MeToo backlash to begin. By January 2018 – just three months after the Weinstein story broke – the question 'Has #MeToo gone too far?' was being bandied around daytime TV sofas and at dinner tables. 'Men simply don't know how to flirt with women anymore,' was a common argument, as was the claim that #MeToo had become a 'witch hunt' for men. On 11 January that year, a group of a hundred French women, including the actress Catherine Deneuve, signed an open letter criticising the movement and defending a man's right to flirt with a woman. They accused #MeToo of fuelling a 'hatred of men and sexuality' and said that a man's 'freedom to pester' women is 'indispensable to sexual freedom', something that many people, me included, couldn't quite understand given that the word 'pester' is literally synonymous with harassment. Regardless, these women argued that #MeToo implied women could not defend themselves against rapists. This, they said, was offensive to female resilience and autonomy, despite the fact that it relies on the stereotypical perception of rape espoused by Weinstein's lawyer, which is that it is easy to avoid so long as you try hard enough.

Of course, conflating flirtation with sexual violence is dangerous. But literally *no one* who has experienced sexual violence, or has a modicum of understanding about it, was doing that. The comments in that letter hark back to another era, one where harassment was so entrenched that it wasn't just tolerated but almost embraced and perceived as flattering. Women were conditioned to view 'pestering' as a part of attraction. We no longer live in that world – thank goodness – and it's up to individuals to differentiate between what constitutes flirtation and sexual harassment. It's really not that difficult and boils down to a case of reading verbal and non-verbal cues. But if people can't make the distinction, then they are part of the reason why we needed the #MeToo movement in the first place.

There have been so many clumsy comments from men in the public eye on this exact topic. Like the actor Taron Egerton, who said that in the wake of #MeToo there are certainly 'situations' where he would 'avoid being alone with certain people'. Why, Taron? In case you accidentally rape them? Or take the time Henry Cavill said 'there's something wonderful about a man chasing a woman', and then made it worse by lamenting 'certain rules' which made such chasing difficult. 'Because then it's like: "Well, I don't want to go up and talk to her, because I'm going to be called a rapist or something."'

Comments like these are not only absurd; they are incredibly dangerous, because they amplify all the damaging myths around rape culture, myths that belittle survivors and absolve perpetrators of guilt and accountability. But as the months rolled on, these comments continued to gain traction, so much so that by November 2018, Burke herself admitted that the #MeToo movement had become 'unrecognisable'. 'Suddenly, a movement to centre survivors of sexual violence is being talked about as a vindictive plot against men,' she told the audience when delivering a TED talk. 'This is a movement about the one in four girls and the one in six boys who are sexually abused every year, and who carry those wounds into adulthood,' she said. 'It's about the far-reaching power of empathy and the millions of people who raised their hands a year ago to say "me too" – and still have their hands raised.' And yet somehow, we got to a place where, as Burke put it, victims of sexual assault are 'heard and then vilified', making #MeToo feel more a moment than a movement.

What is the impact of all this on sex and dating? In order to answer this question, we need to look at two viral stories that emerged in the wake of #MeToo and how they were received. Written by Kristen Roupenian, 'Cat Person' was the short story fronted by the grotesque close-up shot of a kiss that was all over my Twitter and Instagram feed when the *New Yorker* published it in December 2017. It tells the story of Margot, a 20-year-old student working in a cinema, and Robert, a 34-year-old man who may or may not have cats. After an initial spark and some playful texts, the two go on a date that ends awkwardly: Margot decides she doesn't want to have sex with Robert but does so anyway in fear of coming across as 'spoiled and capricious'. Later, she breaks things off, prompting him to send a series of drunken messages that culminate with him calling her a whore.

The story was praised for the way it captured the complexities of desire and repulsion, and how the two can occasionally be strangely fused by lust. But it also highlighted how the fragility of the male ego can affect women in bed. By the time Margot and Robert are on the brink of having sex, she begins to change her mind. But she still has sex with him because she feels it would be impolite to reject him. As Roupenian wrote:

Looking at him like that, so awkwardly bent, his belly thick and soft and covered with hair, Margot recoiled. But the thought of what it would take to stop what she had set in motion was overwhelming; it would require an amount of tact and gentleness that she felt was impossible to summon. It wasn't that she was scared he would try to force her to do something against her will but that insisting that they stop now, after everything she'd done to push this forward, would make her seem spoiled and capricious, as if she'd ordered something at a restaurant and then,

once the food arrived, had changed her mind and sent it
back.

Women loved 'Cat Person'. It struck a chord that they felt
had never before been so much as tickled. There was something
about the way that Margot ricocheted between adolescent-like
yearning and fear – at one point when she's alone with Robert,
she wonders if he might kill her, a nod to Margaret Atwood's
famous quote: 'Men are afraid that women will laugh at them.
Women are afraid that men will kill them.' The story also
highlighted how many expectations we project onto the people
we fancy, which means they often end up disappointing us.
In 'Cat Person', we saw this with the frequent references to
Robert's 'hairy belly', something Margot had not envisioned
in her fantasies about him.

But a lot of men did not love 'Cat Person'. In fact, so
many of them hated it that a Twitter account (@
MenReactToCatPerson) was set up to compile their outrage,
which took aim at the characters in the story as if they were
real people. Here were some of the main gripes:

'She slept with him under false pretences'

'Margot comes off as a borderline sociopath who only cares
about how people perceive her and has little care about
how her actions affect others.'

'Judgemental egotistical girl hooks up with a guy that she
finds physically unattractive. They have sex before they
established any emotional connection. Unsurprisingly the
loveless act is sad and depressing.'

'Cat Person' was not a story about sexual violence. But it added weight to the #MeToo conversation because it was about bad sex, the kind of sex that women have spent years simply rolling over and accepting. Robert did not read Margot's non-verbal cues. Had he asked at any point if she was enjoying herself, what she liked, or if she felt comfortable, things might have been different. Instead, he flips her around like a 'doll', doesn't bother to check if she comes or not, and then collapses on her 'like a tree falling' when he does. The story illustrated how straight women have been taught to expect little from their sexual experiences with men. As Gina Martin said on the podcast: 'There [are] so many different things we worry about and there's such a low bar for what we expect in the bedroom' because there's 'so much that comes before your pleasure'.

However, the fact that 'Cat Person' was included in conversations about #MeToo riled people. It was inevitable, considering the fact that the story came out two months after the movement kicked off. But many people struggled to identify a space in the #MeToo conversation where this story fit. There was no workplace predation, no physical violence and no obvious abuse of power. How then could this be mentioned in the same breath as a story about a Weinstein survivor?

The thing is, even though the sex that Margot and Robert have is consensual, it is unwanted. And while that is obviously less harrowing an experience than rape, to make such a comparison is to miss the point of the #MeToo movement entirely. Just because Robert doesn't rape Margot, does that make the fact that she feels obliged to go through with sex she doesn't want okay? And just because Robert is not Margot's boss, or a high-powered producer, does that mean he doesn't hold any power over her given his age and his greater physical strength?

When I interviewed Roupenian for the *Independent*, she told me that her story 'was powered by #MeToo'. 'But it wasn't like anything had changed,' she added. 'People were just suddenly looking around, like, "Oh my God, things have been really bad for a really long time" and they were hungry for a chance to talk about the uncomfortable stuff they felt they couldn't before.'

There was another story that touched on similar themes to 'Cat Person' and raised similarly uncomfortable conversations – only it wasn't fiction. On 13 January 2018, a website called Babe.com published an article about an anonymous woman, 'Grace', who had been on a date with comedian Aziz Ansari in September 2017. Unlike previous #MeToo stories, this was not about workplace harassment or abuse. It didn't involve a pattern of women sharing stories about a single man. It was a report about a single woman who went out to dinner with a famous comedian she'd met at a party.

The story detailed how Ansari and Grace went out to dinner, where he allegedly plied her with wine, and then took her back to his apartment, where he started making sexual advances towards her. Grace was reticent but claimed that after telling Ansari she didn't 'want to feel forced', he persisted with his advances and in one instance, 'sat back and pointed to his penis and motioned for me to go down on him'. Just as with 'Cat Person', the story went viral. Ansari subsequently released a statement insisting everything between him and Grace was consensual. 'It was true that everything did seem okay to me, so when I heard that it was not the case for her, I was surprised and concerned,' he said. Grace's true identity has never been revealed.

This story was more complex to digest than 'Cat Person',

least of all because it wasn't fictional. First off, it seemed to have been clumsily handled, with Babe having published it within a week of approaching and speaking to Grace, making no apparent attempts to establish a pattern of behaviour from Ansari, as other #MeToo reports had done. Many also raised eyebrows over Grace's credibility, given that Ansari is well-versed in the nuances of modern relationships and the power imbalances between men and women, having written a book on the subject. He also addressed these issues in his comedy, using a set from 2016 to ask the audience to raise their hands if they'd ever come across 'creepy' men. 'That's way too many people,' he replied as many women raised their hands. Of course, none of this means Ansari is not capable of sexual misconduct. But those points alone were enough to make Grace's story one of the most controversial to emerge within the #MeToo movement.

In a piece for the *Washington Post*, writer Sonny Bunch contended that the piece was 'a gift to anyone who wants to derail #MeToo', adding that 'however Grace now thinks of the encounter, what happened isn't sexual assault or anything close to it by most legal or common-sense standards'. Meanwhile, an op-ed writer for *The New York Times*, Bari Weiss, sneered that Grace's story was an 'insidious attempt to criminalize awkward, gross and entitled sex', and *Atlantic* writer Caitlin Flanagan argued that Babe and Grace 'destroyed a man who didn't deserve it' by publishing '3,000 words of revenge porn'.

The issue with all this is that by questioning one woman's right to raise her hand and say 'Me Too', you undermine the entire movement. These comments remove Grace's right to tell her story. They imply that she doesn't have a right to feel violated by what happened to her. I don't know any of those writers, nor do I know whether they've experienced any form of sexual violence. What I do know is that I would be equally critical of Grace's story if something similar had happened to me, and I'd said nothing. Not because I'm saying we should all talk about experiences that we've found violating – some survivors might not ever feel ready to speak up about what happened to them in fear of being retraumatised – but because I would have felt angry for not allowing myself to feel violated. Like I'm angry now that I didn't allow myself to feel violated when that guy put his balls on my face while I was sleeping. It might not have been sexual assault, but that doesn't make it okay, nor does it make it any less valuable to talk about.

'I think it can be dangerous to only include worse case scenarios when discussing sexual harassment, violence and assault,' said Martin, who led the successful campaign to make upskirting illegal in August 2019. 'We have to discuss these more nuanced scenarios because they make up the tapestry of a culture where women don't feel like they are allowed to have agency when it comes to sex, dating and their bodies.' Martin made the point that while of course stories such as 'Cat Person' and those of Grace are different to violent sexual assault and harassment, they are part of the same culture. 'One that allows those who want to violently take advantage of women to do so more easily. When you slowly start to remove agency and autonomy from women over their bodies and their sexuality, you create a culture in which men who are predatory feel validated and thrive.'

That said, Martin told me she would not consider her experience of being upskirted as a part of #MeToo. 'I think using #MeToo as a catch-all for all these stories is reductive. I would say that when #MeToo exploded – six months after I'd started my campaign to make upskirting illegal – it was hugely helpful because it flooded light onto a huge problem and gave context to what I was calling for. I would describe #MeToo as a global movement that acted as a turning point for conversations on sexual assault, not a name for a million different situations.'

Part of the reason why #MeToo became a global movement was thanks to social media, which rewards binary opinions as opposed to nuanced ones. As a result, #MeToo has, to some extent, become less about addressing a culture in which sexual violence and harassment can continue, and more about deciding who does and does not deserve to be a part of the movement, which is why it might be time to move away from using the term altogether. Yes, survivors of sexual violence should continue to speak up if they feel they can. But we have to make room for *every* conversation and give *everyone* the opportunity to have their voice heard, particularly those whose stories are as complex as Grace's. If people don't see those stories as part of the #MeToo movement, then yes, it's time to move beyond it. Because it's only by understanding a wide range of experiences that we will come even close to realising as a society that sexual misconduct is almost never black and white. It is almost always grey, and there's nothing we can do to change that. What we can do, however, is to continue listening to those who have something to say.

Chapter Nine
The Contraception Question

Contraception is one of the worst things about being a woman. I didn't know much about it growing up. I knew about condoms (use them) and I'd heard about the pill (you'll put on weight, but your skin will glow) and that was about it. This was partly down to my naivety and the fact that I wasn't having sex when I was a teenager. And why bother with contraception if you're not having sex? So I didn't, which is why I didn't know that men found wearing condoms uncomfortable. Or that they sometimes took them off without women realising. Or that the morning after pill isn't actually always 100 per cent effective, even if you buy the expensive one and take it twenty minutes after having had unprotected sex. All of which is how I wound up watching Prime Minister's Questions in the waiting room of an abortion clinic, having a panic attack while Theresa May argued with Jeremy Corbyn about the housing market.

Contraception has evolved a lot in recent years. Its history is actually rather fascinating. For example, did you know that women used to insert fruit acids and jellies into their vagina in an attempt to prevent conception? Or that Ancient Egyptian women used – wait for it – crocodile dung? Yes, really. They mixed it with sour milk to create a paste and then inserted it into their vaginas. The idea was that by inserting acidic things into yourself, you create a hostile environment *up there* that sperm wouldn't survive in. Douches were popular, too, at least among Roman women. They would rinse their vaginas before and after sex with things such as lemon juice, sea water, or vinegar in the hope of killing any sperm.

As for condoms, well, those randy Ancient Egyptians are thought to have used linen sheaths, not to prevent pregnancy, but to prevent the contracting of tropical diseases during sex. Ancient Romans, meanwhile, created condoms out of animal intestines, a technique that remained popular until the eighteenth century. It wasn't until 1843 that rubber condoms came about. In the 1930s, rubber was replaced with latex – which is formed when rubber is dispersed in water – and then in 1997, the first polyurethane condom launched in the UK. It was the discovery of AIDS in the 1980s that led to the popularity of condoms both as a contraceptive and as a way of preventing sexually transmitted diseases.

The rest of the more complex contraception methods – more on those later – were mostly developed in the 1900s. But the real humdinger was the pill. While oral contraceptives date back 2,000 years – when everything from willow shoots to bees were consumed – the pill was a complete gamechanger. Brought to the UK in 1961, the pill catalysed the great sexual revolution of the twentieth century. At the time, it was mainly prescribed to older women who did not want any more children – the government didn't want to be seen as promoting promiscuity. But then, in 1974, family planning clinics were permitted to offer the pill to single women. And so finally women were allowed to copulate freely, which is perhaps why an advert for one of the first pill brands – Enovid – was fronted by an image of the Greek goddess Andromeda who, like all British women, was suddenly freed from her societal chains.

Today, there are so many different types of contraception that it's hard to keep track. In the UK, there are now fifteen different methods available to women and people of minority genders who menstruate. But there are also countless varieties of each type. Take the pill, for example. There are pills you take for twenty-one days with a seven-day break, and there are pills you take continuously. There are pills that have oestrogen and progesterone and there are pills with only progesterone. There are pills that might give you spots and some that might give you headaches. And then there are pills that might give you something else entirely, like a mental health condition.

In recent years, mounting evidence has found links between the pill and depression. The NHS is still hesitant to confirm these links, stating only that there 'may' be a correlation, but that further research is needed to confirm this. The journalist Vicky Spratt has written extensively about her experience of having mental health issues on the pill and explored this in depth on a BBC Two documentary in 2018. After taking it aged 14, Spratt explained she started suffering from depression and experienced panic attacks. 'I remember thinking "if this is what the rest of my life is going to be like, I don't want to live it",' she recalled in the documentary. Spratt was prescribed antidepressants and cognitive behavioural therapy, but not one doctor or psychologist made the link between her deteriorating mental state and the contraceptive pill. After stumbling upon some articles that linked the pill to depression, Spratt stopped taking it. She felt better 'within weeks'.

My friend Lulu had a similar experience when she went on the mini pill, aka a progesterone-only pill. 'It really affected me mentally. I would stand in the mirror and cry all day,' she recalled. 'I was really horrible to my boyfriend, too. We nearly broke up because of it – then I realised that the pill could be to blame for the change in my behaviour, so I came off it. And I was a completely different person. It was so odd.'

We spoke about the many side effects women have to put up with when they take contraception on the podcast with the podcaster Oenone Forbat, who spoke about how she believes the pill gave her mild depression after a break-up. 'I've never had depression or been diagnosed, but there were times when I felt in a depressive mood and had lowered feelings,' she explained. 'And I've never had those feelings since coming off the pill. It's hard because I've spoken to doctors who've said there's no correlation, but it's really hard to deny it because I know so many people who've had similar experiences.'

I want to highlight how common experiences like these are, and not just in terms of the pill and how it impacts people mentally. But how the entire smorgasbord of contraceptives – implants, coils, injection and all – can take a major physical and emotional toll on so many people. I put a call out on social media asking for stories, here are just a few of them.

The implant made me nuts. I threw a plate at the wall because I was so angry at my partner. I came off it and have never done anything like that since.

I used to get intense nausea and heart palpitations from my pill. As soon as I came off it, the symptoms dissipated.

I had to get my copper coil taken out because it was making my hairline thinner due to 'copper toxicity', I didn't even know that was a thing. My sexual health doctor didn't seem to know either.

I had a hormonal coil put in and it partially fell out when I was in the shower. I had to go and get it removed properly in the sexual health clinic, it was so painful.

After I gave birth to my first child, I got a hormonal coil put in. A few weeks later I went for a cervical smear test and they couldn't find the coil. It had gone missing inside me. No one could find it. Fast forward two years and I had surgery to get it taken out. It transpired that the coil had gone up to my large intestine and attached itself there. The doctor explained that after having had a baby, my uterus would have been very soft, too soft to have a coil. I wish someone had told me that at the sexual health clinic.

I lost nearly two stone in the first six months of being on the hormonal coil. I also developed acne and started to get very heavy periods. I went to my doctor and they said that acne is an 'almost inevitable' side effect of my coil – something they hadn't told me before I had it put in – and while weight loss is rare, it does happen. I then started to bleed very heavily after sex, to the point where I once had to spend twenty minutes cleaning myself up in the toilet while on a night out. I went back to the doctor to have the coil removed and they discovered that it had actually scarred my uterus to an extent that any pressure in that area was

*likely to cause intense bleeding. Now, nearly a year later,
I'm still having problems with bleeding.*

With all these stories, and those I'm sure you've heard or
maybe experienced yourself, it's no wonder some people choose
to forgo contraception altogether. Some prefer to use condoms
while others favour the famous 'pull-out method' – this is
medically known as the 'withdrawal method' and is when a
man withdraws his penis before ejaculating during sex. More
recently, though, some people choosing to shun contraception
have sought out more contemporary alternatives, such as
fertility apps. These are smartphone apps that allow users to
track their menstrual cycle under the premise that you can
then track when you can and cannot have unprotected sex
without getting pregnant. The most well-known of these is
an app called Natural Cycles, which proudly states that it is
the only fertility app to have been approved by the Food and
Drug Administration.

On the podcast, Forbat explained that she started using
Natural Cycles because she was scared to go back on hormonal
contraception in light of how the pill had affected her mood.
But going hormone-free is not as blissful as it sounds. In fact,
it's quite complicated. Most fertility apps, Natural Cycles
included, require you to take your temperature the second you
wake up. I'm talking before you've even had a sip of water, let
alone before you've done a morning wee. You then have to put
your temperature into the app, which will then make a predic-
tion about your fertility for the day. On Natural Cycles, green
means you can have unprotected sex. Red means you can't,
unless you want to get pregnant.

If you use Natural Cycles completely accurately, it claims

to be 99 per cent effective as a contraceptive. This means that one in 100 women using the app as contraception will get pregnant. However, with regular imperfect use – i.e. with room for human error – according to studies carried out by the company, that figure drops to 93 per cent, meaning seven in every 100 women will get pregnant. Natural Cycles became embroiled in controversy in 2018 when 37 women from a single hospital in Sweden reported unwanted pregnancies after using the app, leading them all to seek abortions. Natural Cycles responded that the number of pregnancies was proportional to the registered number of Swedish users and was 'in line' with its expectations. An investigation conducted by the Swedish Medical Products Agency confirmed this.

But many people still had doubts over whether a smartphone app could ever accurately predict a woman's fertility. These doubts were validated when, in an interview in the *Guardian*, Natural Cycle's co-founder Elina Berglund described her ideal user as a woman who wanted a break from hormonal contraception, but also wanted to have children at some point – a message not clearly expressed in the company's marketing, which focused solely on the fact that Natural Cycles was a hormone-free contraceptive. Had Berglund's ideal user been mentioned in any one of the glossy social media influencer's posts about the service, it would have put some women off. Women who, like writer Olivia Sudjic, simply wanted a contraceptive that wouldn't wildly alter their bodies or minds with a cocktail of side effects. 'I got pregnant when the predictions of fertile and infertile changed back and forth in one day, turning from green to red, *after* I had unprotected sex,' Sudjic wrote in the *Guardian*, revealing she had an abortion. 'I put so much faith in a technology that in the end relied on something as unreliable as my body. What's the hashtag for that?'

I've painted a fairly bleak picture thus far. But contraception *is* bleak. At least, it can be until you find the right one for you. For some people, it might be as straightforward as trying one pill and staying on it for much of your adult life. The pill can be a godsend for some, as can many of the other forms of contraception I've criticised thus far. It just depends on how an individual's body responds; some people are simply luckier than others. I'm on the hormonal coil now, and it's mostly fine aside from the fact that I get incredibly sore breasts in the week before my period. And yes, I still get my period, even though the doctor told me I wouldn't anymore. But considering some of the stories outlined above, I'm in no position to complain about such minor side effects.

Let's look at the bigger picture here. The most galling thing about all this is that while so many people have to go through hell and back to find a form of contraception that doesn't make them crazy, spotty or suicidal, all any man has to do is slip on a condom. Contraception is a sexist issue, whether we like it or not. We spoke about this on the podcast with Sophie Mackintosh, author of *The Water Cure* and *Blue Ticket*, whose books examine motherhood and female bodily autonomy. 'I really resent that men have it so easy,' she said, pointing out how many men refuse to even wear condoms, something that has become a widely accepted fact. We've all heard the excuses. Condoms are uncomfortable. They are desensitising. They don't fit.

A recent survey found that just one-third of men use

condoms 'some of the time' when they have sex.* 'It seems insane to me that a man would just willingly get you pregnant for his own pleasure,' Mackintosh said when we discussed the universal male reluctance to condom-wearing. 'Contraception is seen as a woman's responsibility,' she added. Of course, women are the ones who carry children. And I'm sure there are many people who would argue that this fact alone renders contraception a woman's responsibility. But that's not completely fair, is it? Why should women be the ones that have to put up with mental and physical turmoil to solve a problem that men not only help create, but have the power to fix in seconds?

But the sexism surrounding contraception runs deeper still. On the podcast, Mackintosh recalled how she was experiencing some weird side effects on the mini pill. 'My male GP was so uninterested and was like, "well, you just have to sort of put up with it or change". And then I saw a female GP who was like, "it's not acceptable for this to be happening to you". She gave me another pill to take with my actual pill that somehow stopped all the side effects.' Mackintosh went back to her male GP and asked why he hadn't suggested this sooner. 'He said he had no idea how the drug interaction worked.'

Gender bias has a major impact on contraception. 'This has been happening literally since the day the pill was invented,' said Alice Pelton, founder of The Lowdown, the world's first review platform for contraceptives. 'In 1956, Dr Gregory Goodwin Pincus and Dr John Rock conducted large scale clinical trials of the first pill on two hundred women in Puerto Rico. The pills they tested contained ten times the amount of

---

* National Center of Health Statistics, 2017.

hormones in today's pills, and the women weren't told they were taking part in a trial or about any of the risks they'd face.' When the women began to experience side effects such as nausea, headaches and blood clots, their complaints were dismissed, and the women were labelled unreliable. This remains the case for many women today. 'Countless women at The Lowdown complain about unwanted non-life threatening side effects that really impact their general wellbeing,' said Pelton. 'Society has come to accept this, the same way we accept car accidents. But contraception is used by over one billion women worldwide, and the average woman uses it for thirty years. It's not a short-term thing. And we must remember that these women are unlikely to be taking contraception because they are *ill* [though this might be the case for some] – this is not medication. We're not killing cancer. Our acceptance of side effects and understanding of contraception needs to change to reflect that.'

From the reviews it has received so far, The Lowdown has found that 78 per cent of women experience side effects from their contraception. Half say their contraception has impacted their wellbeing and mental health and another half of women say that contraception has specifically negatively impacted their mood. On top of all that, 30 per cent of The Lowdown's users feel that their doctor doesn't listen to or understand their contraceptive needs.

One way to address many of the issues with contraception would be to introduce a male contraceptive. Sadly, it doesn't look like this will happen any time soon. Trials have been ongoing for years, but there's no sign of anything making it to market yet. There was a fairly successful year-long trial of a male contraceptive in 2016, but that was stopped by researchers when 20 of the 320 participants dropped out of the trial because they were experiencing too many side effects, including acne, increased libido and mood disorders – all of which, by the way, are side effects for female contraceptives. However, the side effects were judged to have been so 'unacceptable' by researchers that they had no choice but to stop the trial. This was despite the results showing it was effective at stopping pregnancy in over 96 per cent of couples.

Allen Pacey, professor of andrology at the University of Sheffield, told me that while there is one clinical trial looking at a new contraceptive gel for men, and a small amount of research being conducted by the Gates Foundation into drug screenings for possible contraceptive targets, there has been 'very little' research into finding a male contraceptive. 'I can't see any new male contraceptives making it to market any time soon,' Pacey told me. 'My understanding is that there is little interest from pharmaceutical companies in this area.'

There are wider societal inequalities to consider with all this, too. While sexual health workers are now being trained in delivering healthcare to transgender and non-binary people, it can still be difficult for these individuals to access contraception. Elsewhere, studies have found that black women are more likely than white women to use contraceptive methods with lower efficacy, a figure which makes them three times as likely to experience unplanned pregnancy.*

When I spoke to sexual and reproductive health doctor Dr Annabel Sowemimo about the reason for this, she pointed out that cultural differences play an important role in sexual

---

* Seeking Causes for Race-Related Disparities in Contraceptive Use, *AMA Journal of Ethics*, October 2014.

healthcare, particularly when it comes to how long-acting methods of contraception are viewed in certain communities. 'Different cultures have different belief systems around reproduction,' she said. 'In my Nigerian culture, for example, people pray for me to have children, even if that's not in my plans. It's seen as a beautiful thing for people to bestow on me. So when you start considering using something that will suppress your fertility, a lot of people come from homes where that's not seen as a good thing. I was told by my family that long-acting contraception could make me infertile.'

The trouble is that these factors aren't taken into account when sexual healthcare is being researched, which is not surprising considering how little research has been done. These are just some of the reasons why Dr Sowemimo launched Decolonising Contraception, an advocacy group that addresses the barriers that minority groups face when it comes to accessing sexual healthcare.

'I have no doubt that the lack of interest in sexual reproduction as a whole is racist, sexist and homophobic, which is why it doesn't get the interest it deserves in terms of how much it affects people's lives,' said Dr Sowemimo. 'On top of that, there are the judgements people want to place on people having sex, and viewing people's sex lives as promiscuous, all of which has an impact on why funding in the sector has been decimated in the last ten years.'

Let's talk about sexually transmitted diseases. Condoms are the only form of contraception that can prevent pregnancy and protect you from STIs, which is just one of the reasons why it's so baffling when men refuse to wear them. Despite what you might have heard or read, STIs are no picnic. Whether it's chlamydia, gonorrhoea or genital herpes, the symptoms can be brutal. Like thick green discharge, pain during sex, vaginal bleeding, blisters and rashes. STIs are incredibly common. Public Health England estimates that a young person is diagnosed with either chlamydia or gonorrhoea every four minutes in England and 50 per cent of sexually active people will have at least one STI by the age of 25. And yet, despite their ubiquity, STIs remain shrouded in stigma.

And so we don't really talk about them. Not among our friends, and certainly not to a new sexual partner, even though this is exactly who we should be talking to about STIs. It's just so bloody awkward, isn't it? Picture the scene. You've just had a wonderful third date with a hot person. For the sake of gender-neutrality (because anyone can get an STI), let's call them Jo. Jo is really hot. Like Hollywood hot. You want to sleep with Jo. In fact, you've wanted to sleep with Jo ever since you saw their Hinge profile. So when the moment comes, and you're four gin and tonics deep, you're undressing quickly and fervidly. There is no talk of condoms, and when Jo starts putting their hand down your pants, you don't want to ruin the moment by asking them when their last STI test was. The next morning, you wake up and your genitals are sore. You think nothing of it. A few months pass, and you're experiencing irregular discharge. It's yellow. You're still sore. You assume it's nothing serious. More months pass. The pain persists. Finally, you go to the doctor. It transpires you've had chlamydia ever since you slept with Jo and that you're now infertile.

This is a worse-case scenario. But it's so important that we tackle the stigma surrounding STIs, because research has found that it actually prevents people from getting tested, thus leading to an increase in the spread of infection. And while many

STIs can be treated easily with a course of antibiotics and may even be symptomless, when they are left untreated, they can become very serious indeed. Some, like chlamydia, can render you infertile. Others can lead to pelvic inflammatory disease or reactive arthritis. So why don't we talk about them more? And why are people so reluctant to get tested?

The difficulty is that people wrongly associate STIs with promiscuity. And even though this makes no logical sense – it only takes having unprotected sex once to give you an STI – it's a misconception that isn't going away any time soon. Writing in *The New York Times*, obstetrician and gynaecologist Jen Gunter explained that she receives hundreds of questions from people on Twitter about almost everything to do with sexual health apart from STIs. 'It seems STIs are one of the last taboos,' she wrote. 'I see this reflected in my day-to-day work. No diagnosis, apart from cancer, can as reliably bring a woman to tears as an STI.' Given the way that society views female sexuality – see Chapter Six – it does not surprise me that women might feel more shame when they contract an STI than men. Contracting one, as Gunter wrote, makes women feel like 'damaged goods'.

There is no clear explanation to this. But it is worth pointing out that STIs are generally higher in marginalised groups – women, people of colour and those in the LGBT+ community – where shame is weaponised as a form of oppression. This is thanks to 'a combination of biology', said Gunter, 'as transmission to the cervix, vagina and rectum is easiest for most STIs, and traditionally people in these groups have less access to health care because of economic marginalisation or prejudice, which leads to less access to screening and treatment'.

The stigma that surrounds STIs has affected me personally.

It's the reason why, when I got chlamydia in 2018, I never found out who gave it to me, because neither one of the two men it could have been would admit they had it. It was no big deal, symptoms-wise. Just a bit of pain and some random bleeding. But the timing could not have been worse. Let me explain.

I met George in the summer. We'd been on two wonderful dates – one to see a film about sharks at the cinema, another at a waterside pub in King's Cross – but we hadn't slept together yet. We'd talked about everything on our dates: our families, our careers, our ambitions. He was attractive, charming and kind; I immediately felt comfortable around him. But there was a problem. Two weeks before I'd started dating George, I'd slept with a 23-year-old in France. He was a friend of a friend, and while he was absolutely not my type – he posted selfies on his Instagram captioned with '#mood' – he was a welcome distraction while I was getting over an ex. Foolishly, we didn't use a condom. I ordered an at-home STI test when I got back to London, but I was still waiting for the results when I slept with George for the first time. Again, we didn't use a condom. This was dumb and selfish. Very dumb and very selfish. But I really liked George, and there are few things less sexy than telling someone you really like that you can't have sex because you might have an STI. In hindsight, I've realised that nothing is sexier than safe sex, but I was naive.

The day after we had sex, I was in a good mood. I went to a café in central London to celebrate my blossoming relationship with George over an overpriced acai bowl. I was midway through a chunk of granola when the text came through from Sexual Health London. My results. I clicked on the link. The words flashed onto my screen like a tabloid headline. Chlamydia: positive. I yelped, choked on my granola, and then Googled 'how do you give someone chlamydia?', in the hope that maybe I'd got it wrong all these years and that maybe chlamydia was a weird science-defying kind of STI that you can't pass to someone through sex. Reader, it is not. I texted George.

> Me: Hi, um, I hate to tell you this. But I just got the result of an STI test. And while I very ambitiously thought I would be fine, it transpires that I have chlamydia.
> George: If anyone was ever going to give me chlamydia, I'm pleased it was you.
> Me: I'm touched.
> George: Livi, I really like you; this is going to be nipped in the bud. No dramas.

George's response made me like him even more (how could he be *this* nice?). He immediately went to the sexual health clinic and got a course of antibiotics. I didn't have much time to indulge in my swooning. Now that I knew I had chlamydia, I had to get in touch with the last two people I'd slept with, as I'd obviously caught it from one of them. I called up the ex – one of the most awkward phone conversations in my life – and he kindly offered to get tested. Then I DM'd the 23-year-old on Instagram. 'Bonjour, so I just got an STI test back and I have chlamydia. Telling you because I either gave it to you or you gave it to me. You should probably get tested. Au revoir.' Putting French words in there somehow made me feel like the message would be more charming. But apparently it wasn't because he replied bluntly that he took a test last week and was clean. The ex told me his test was also clean. Something was amiss. Thanks to my curious Google search, I now know with certainty that you do in fact contract chlamydia from sex. You don't simply get it from walking into Agent Provocateur. So, one of them was clearly lying to me, either out of embarrassment or maybe even out of shame.

Shame shapes so many conversations we have around sexual health beyond that which surrounds STIs and female sexuality. Take emergency contraception. This is the kind of contraception you take after having had unprotected sex. There are two types: the emergency contraceptive pill (often referred to as the 'morning after pill') and the intrauterine device (IUD). The former is more common – I didn't even know the latter existed until I started the podcast – and is the one that is often stigmatised and mythologised. Even the name is deceptive. There are two types of emergency contraceptive pills and they can be taken a few days after intercourse, not just 'the morning after'. While both are more effective the sooner you take them, ellaOne can be taken up to five days after unprotected sex and levonorgestrel can be taken for up to three days.

But the name 'morning after pill' is more problematic still when you consider other words it has become synonymous with. When you think of the 'morning after', it conjures up words such as 'regret', 'irresponsible' and 'loose'. It is a phrase that is synonymous with debauchery and casual sex, which, again, is completely nonsensical given that there are an endless number of scenarios that would leave you seeking emergency contraception, including a condom breaking during sex with a long-term partner, for example. As for where this sense of shame comes from, may I remind you that the majority of people taking emergency contraception identify as women. And so again, I bring you back to society's warped understanding of female sexuality which dictates that a woman who has sexual autonomy – at least to the degree whereby she has unprotected sex and needs emergency contraception – is disgusting, dangerous and must be oppressed.

The consequences of this become even more complex when we consider what happens when contraception of any kind – emergency or otherwise – fails. In the UK, an unwanted pregnancy can be dealt with in one of two ways. You can choose to stay pregnant and have a child, or you can choose to have an abortion, which one in three women in the UK will have in their lifetime. Having the ability to make that choice is an enormous privilege, one that women in the Republic of Ireland and Northern Ireland have only recently been granted.

In the US, abortion remains a highly contentious issue and is restricted in many states. In May 2019, the state of Alabama even passed a bill to ban abortion outright, including in cases of incest and rape, and punish doctors who administer them with life imprisonment. Meanwhile, five other states (Georgia, Ohio, Kentucky, Mississippi and Louisiana) have all passed bills that prohibit abortions after six weeks, which is before many women even know they're pregnant. This was all partly thanks to the leadership of Donald Trump, who made his anti-abortion stance clear through various incidents, such as when he became the first sitting president to speak at the annual March for Life rally in Washington in January 2020. Or when, in 2017, he reinstated a 'global gag rule' policy that prohibited any overseas organisation that received US global health funding from even mentioning abortion as part of its education programmes.

Then there is the devastatingly long list of countries where abortion is only legal on the basis of health or therapeutic grounds (Poland, Colombia, Morocco), or when the woman's life is at risk (Mexico, Brazil, Indonesia). And, of course, there are also those countries where it is completely illegal altogether. This list includes Madagascar, Jamaica, Egypt and the Philippines.

Even in the UK, where abortion has been legal since 1967, it is still technically classified as a criminal act according to a Victorian law that only renders abortion lawful if two doctors agree that continuing with a pregnancy would affect a woman's mental or physical health. Various campaigns have been launched to combat this and decriminalise abortion in the UK.

The issue will always be that restricting or criminalising abortions does not stop women from having or needing them. It simply makes them more dangerous, as people will seek underground terminations that pose serious health and safety threats. The World Health Organization estimates that twenty-five million unsafe abortions take place each year, the majority of which are in developing countries. The organisation describes them as 'a procedure for terminating an unintended pregnancy carried out either by persons lacking the necessary skills or in an environment that does not conform to minimal medical standards, or both'.

This all contributes to the stigma that surrounds abortion to this day. And unlike other taboos, that are slowly being dismantled, the stigma attached to abortion seems to only be growing in momentum in recent years. 'I think there's more shame attached to abortion now,' the writer and pro-choice campaigner Polly Vernon told me, explaining that this is partly thanks to the advent of social media, which has given a greater platform to anti-abortion campaigners. If you haven't heard them on Twitter, though, you might see them in the flesh if you visit an abortion clinic in the UK, where protesters stand outside and try to dissuade women from going through with their terminations. They will pray, hold vigils and offer leaflets packed with misinformation about abortion and pictures of foetuses. While some clinics have since implemented buffer zones, which prevent protesters from coming within 100 metres of the clinic's doors, a parliamentary inquiry to make these compulsory across England and Wales was rejected by the government.

The only way to combat the stigma surrounding abortion is to speak openly about it, as Vernon has done. The *Hot Feminist* author has spoken extensively about having had three abortions in her late teens and early twenties, revealing they were 'shame free' and 'regret free'. 'I feel like the nineties and early 2000s were probably more progressive in terms of abortion rights, and we may have gone backwards,' she told me.

But while Vernon explained she has never felt shame about her terminations, she has felt some pressure to explain the reasons behind them. 'Which is weird, cos truly: it's no one else's business,' she added. 'Two of my pregnancies resulted from things now recognised as crimes. The first time, my partner removed a condom halfway through and didn't tell me for a week, at which point, it was too late for me to take the morning after pill. This is now considered rape, sexual assault at the very least, though it wasn't at the time.' She continued:

The second pregnancy was in the context of an abusive relationship, I was being horribly controlled by my then boyfriend, I was really scared of him: refusing to use contraception was just one of his weapons of choice for control. This is also now a legally recognised expression of coercive control. I don't think women should ever have to justify their abortions beyond: shit happens. Yet I still feel compelled to explain! I really hope we get to a point where I, and women like me, who've also had more than one abortion, don't. But that's the extent of my shame. Mainly, I've felt relief and gratitude about being able to make those choices and mounting anger that many women still can't.

From the moment Vernon started speaking openly about her abortions, she realised how much she needed to do so. 'The very act of openness frees up other women hugely. Because I'm loud and proud, irreverent and funny about abortion, because I like to overturn the drama and stigma generally attached to abortion, the idea this is The Hardest Decision A Woman Ever Has To Make (is it bugger! I have a harder time choosing sandwiches in Pret), people really respond to that. I've had so many emails and DMs from women saying I made them feel OK about their abortions for the first time ever . . . I think that's by far the most important thing I'll ever achieve in my writing.'

I've always felt so inspired by how open Vernon is about her abortions. And how open other public figures and celebrities have been, particularly in the wake of the spate of anti-abortion restrictions being passed in US states and during the Repeal the Eighth campaign. Everyone from Jemima Kirke, Nicki Minaj, Cathy Newman and Whoopi Goldberg have spoken publicly about their terminations. Meanwhile, social media campaigns have continued to encourage women to do the same, such as #ShoutYourAbortion, #SmashAbortionStigma and #YouKnowMe, which was launched in May 2019 after the actor Busy Philipps asked women who had had abortions to 'share their truth' by posting their story on Twitter. The hashtag soon went viral, proving just how desperate women who'd had abortions were to de-stigmatise them.

It was about three weeks after I'd slept with Henry that I realised I might be pregnant. I always knew it was a possibility given that, as I alluded to at the start of this chapter, he'd taken the condom off when we were having sex without my consent. And yes, as Vernon said, that is sexual assault, though I didn't realise that at the time. Henry told me what had happened when he'd returned from the toilet a few minutes after. He explained that he thought it would be more comfortable for both of us and that I must have realised. Henry offered to split the price of the morning after pill with me, but I had to go to the pharmacy alone and in the next five minutes, because he had a train to catch.

Henry was only the third person I'd slept with, and the first one that I actually saw some sort of future with. He was insanely clever to the point where I'd inhale every word he said and then regurgitate it to friends as if he was some sort of oracle. I never questioned anything he told me, not just because I assumed he knew better, but also because I was afraid that if I did, he'd realise I wasn't half as smart as he was. So ingrained was this, that when Henry told me what he'd done that night, I blamed my lack of sexual experience.

I was reluctant to get a pregnancy test. Partly because I was in denial, but mostly because I had no idea what I'd do if it was positive. None of my friends had had abortions, at least not to my knowledge, and I didn't have a clue where to even get one, or how they worked. Again, this was not something I was taught at school. But thanks to the encouragement of friends and a very sweet woman down the phone when I called 111 in a panic, I mustered up the strength to buy a test on my lunch break at work. The plan was to take it at home, but my mind was racing far too much to wait. I locked myself in a cubicle at the gym near my office and took the test there.

I texted my Cock Warriors WhatsApp group: 'Okay so I'm about to take a pregnancy test. £5 in Boots for two, bargain. Any of you around please make yourselves known.' Ella replied immediately. 'I'm here.' The others soon followed. I peed on the stick and wondered whether anyone else had ever taken a pregnancy test in their gym's toilets before. The line turned red and I realised I had no idea what that meant – I checked the back of the packet. 'Guys, I've taken one test and it says that means I'm pregnant. I'm hoping it's wrong. Going to take another one.' I took the other one. Another red line. 'Both saying positive. What do I do?'. Ella told me to buy a more expensive test. 'Fuck this isn't good,' wrote Lexi. 'Get ClearBlue, that's the best one. It just says "pregnant or not pregnant". None of this line shit.' I went back to Boots and bought the ClearBlue test. In the spirit of variety, I decided to take it in the toilet in a nearby WholeFoods: 'Pregnant, two to three weeks.'

I went into action mode and spent the next forty-five minutes pacing around the streets behind my office. Google told me to phone the British Pregnancy Advisory Service

(BPAS). BPAS told me there was a three-week waitlist and I should try Marie Stopes. Marie Stopes put me on their wait-list. I was meant to be flying to San Francisco the following week to see my dad. Our relationship is fractious at the best of times, so the thought of telling him I had to cancel my trip to get an abortion was unbearable. As was the thought of allowing something I desperately wanted to ignore grow inside me for another three weeks. I found a private clinic that could see me in two days' time – it would cost £650. Thankfully, I had saved a bit of money over the years from tutoring A level English to local teenagers – though I'd envis-aged spending it on a holiday to Greece rather than an abortion.

When I told Henry over the phone, he was predictably blasé. Frankly, I was just grateful he didn't try to talk me out of it. He offered to come to the clinic with me and I told him not to – I couldn't bear the thought of crying while he mumbled platitudes about nihilism. A few minutes after we'd said goodbye, he sent me a text. 'Hey, hope you're okay. Sorry you're going through this, it's such an arbitrary burden. You're so strong, you'll be completely fine.' I Googled 'arbitrary' and tried to figure out why he'd used that word. I'm still not entirely sure.

Lola, of my Cock Warriors WhatsApp group, came with me to the clinic and squeezed my hand tightly when the nurse did the ultrasound to confirm that I was in fact pregnant. I was given the choice between a surgical and medical abortion. The former, I was told, would take just twenty minutes and would require local anaesthetic. The latter would mean taking two tablets one day apart; there would be quite a lot of bleeding. Surgery sounded dramatic, so I chose the medical

option. I was given one pill at the clinic and then returned
the next day for the second – this was the one that would
kickstart the abortion. The nurse inserted it into my vagina.
'Right, all done,' she said, as if she'd just waxed my legs.

My oldest friend, Allie, picked me up in her car and drove
me straight to her house – I was living with family at the
time and didn't want to tell them. So I spent the afternoon
watching *Grey's Anatomy* at Allie's with a hot water bottle on
my belly. She dropped me home in the evening. I was alone.
Naturally, that's when the pain started. I'd been given some
painkillers at the clinic, but they didn't seem to do anything.
It felt like someone, or *something*, was repeatedly punching
the lower part of my stomach and twisting every organ until
it burst. The lining of my womb was breaking down. I ran
to the toilet and noticed that dark, thick blood was spilling
over my sanitary towel and dripping onto the floor. I stood
in the bath, T-shirt on, pants off, and gradually collapsed into
a crouching position. Every part of me was writhing in agony,
and the puddle of blood below me had widened. That's when
I saw it. A fleshy globule no larger than a baked bean. Buried
in blood, it was sticky and small. I touched it, and then I
vomited.

After the abortion, all I wanted to do was talk about it. I
wanted to understand what had happened to me and what
was going to happen next. I couldn't talk to Henry, because
he ended things with me when I returned from San Francisco.
I couldn't talk to my family, because I was terrified of what
they might think. And while I did talk to my friends, there
was only so much they could comfort me given that none of
them had experienced an abortion. So, I turned to the internet
and spent hours scouring the web for stories of abortions from

other women. I needed someone to tell me how this was supposed to feel because nothing I felt made sense. One minute it was guilt, the next it was humiliation. Then it was relief and giddy joy. And then there was the constant feeling of emptiness.

Despite my avid Googling, I couldn't find a single article about abortion written by a woman who had had one. There were plenty of news items and a few tweets, but nothing that discussed in any depth about how the termination had impacted them physically and mentally. How it could give you violent tears one moment and propel you into a violent rage blackout minutes later. I had nothing to compare my experience to and no way to make sense of it. And so for a long time, it didn't make sense.

Thankfully, it's finally beginning to. Today, thanks to the aforementioned campaigns, there are stories about abortions across the internet, many of which I'm sure will help women who, like me, only got closer to understanding their own experience by reading those of others. Because whether it's abortion, sexual harassment, or even something more inane like read receipt anxiety, everything feels so much harder when you think you're the only one going through it. But you aren't. In fact, you almost never are.

A Few Final Words

This is the part where I'm supposed to write something profound. I'm supposed to tell you how much I've learned in the process of writing this book, how far I've come on my own path to love and how I've succeeded in becoming a content philosophically literate unicorn that knows exactly what she wants – and how to get it. But I am not a unicorn. And neither are you.

Quite a lot has happened since I started writing this book. The pandemic has ripped through the social fabric of our lives and, as I write this, it's still not clear when it will be stitched back together again, or if it ever will be. At least not in the way it was before. Loved ones have been lost, careers put on hold and relationships have been ravaged, including my own.

The break-up I went through reshaped everything I thought I knew about love. In fact, what it mainly did was highlight how little I know, and how much I have to learn. I made some terrible decisions in the months that followed, ones I never thought I'd make. Like sleeping with a stranger on the bathroom floor of another stranger's home. And convincing myself that someone I'd slept with twice was going to fall in love with me (and telling him as much) despite the fact he never even gave me his phone number. I also wore the same matching tracksuit top and bottoms for almost ten days, which is a bit off-topic, but it's still not something I'm proud of.

The point is that I've made mistakes. And I'm sure I'll make a few more, as I suspect you might. That's just how it works. Everything is a learning curve when it comes to love, especially when you're in your twenties and thirties. There's so much at stake, so many milestones we've been told to hit – and we tell ourselves when to hit them.

We say things like: 'I'll meet the love of my life at 27', 'I'll be onto my second kid at 31' and 'I'll get married in the Cotswolds when I'm 34 and drink a shit ton of rosé'. But if 2020 taught us anything, it's that nothing is certain. You can't create a blueprint for your life, let alone your love life. And putting pressure on yourself to meet deadlines for things you don't even know you want yet will backfire. It always does.

Some unexpected things that have happened in my own love life: I stopped pining after someone I thought I was meant to be with; the man I gave an STI to ended up being the first person I fell in love with; and, after years of insisting I didn't need it, I finally went into therapy – try telling a relationships counsellor that you're writing a book about relationships.

If I've learned one lesson through all this, it's that the most important thing is to work out what it really is that you want from love and why you want it. We've been conditioned to want to find our 'soul mate'. That one perfect person who completes us – see the (awful) phrase 'other half' – and who will meet all of our needs and desires. But that's a completely unrealistic ambition, one that will only leave you feeling disappointed every time you enter into a relationship. As woo woo as it may sound, the only person who can complete us is, well, us.

What kind of relationship are you looking for? And what role do you want that relationship to have in your life? What kind of romantic partner do you want to be? And how will you become that person?

I'm 27, and while I like to think I know myself, these are all questions I'm still asking. There are, however, some things that I'm fairly certain of: the quality that matters most in a romantic partner is kindness, consent is everything, trying to work out who your ex is talking to when they come 'online' on WhatsApp will stop you from sleeping, pizza always tastes better the next day, Fuck Boys stop being Fuck Boys the moment you stop thinking about them, the best relationships are the ones that exist only in your head and it's cool to care. Try to remember that last one the next time you punish yourself for simply being yourself. I know I will.

Acknowledgements

If you've skipped to this part before reading the book, I get it. I do this, too. This isn't really a spoiler kind of book but I'll bear you in mind even so.

There are a lot of people without whom this book would never have happened. The first is my wonderful editor, Michelle Kane. I'm so happy you slid into my DMs. Your unrelenting support and belief in me means everything. Thank you to everyone else at 4th Estate who has worked tirelessly on this book – it has been a privilege to work with all of you and I'm so honoured to be one of your authors.

None of this would have happened without *Millennial Love*, the podcast, for which I have many people to thank. My old boss, Dave Maclean, who was the one that asked Rachel Hosie and I to 'start a podcast about dating' as part of our roles at the *Independent*. Chloe Hubbard, who convinced me to continue the podcast even after Rachel had left. Tom Richell, my patient producer and friend, who once asked me to start editing the show and then silently started editing it himself again once he realised how crap I was at it. Thank you to everyone else at the *Independent* for your support and encouragement. And back to Rachel. We started the podcast together; I'll never forget how kind you were when I told you about this project. I also want to thank all of the wonderful people who have shared their stories with me, both for the podcast and for this book. Your generosity means everything to me.

Thank you to my friends and family, so many of whom put me up when I was writing this book. I'd particularly like to mention Natalie Greenwold, Nanou Onona, Allie Miller, Chloe Taylor-Gee, Lutia Swan-Hutton and Patrick Smith. I must also thank the Cock Warriors (Ella McMahon, Lexi Allan, Bethan Jones and Lola Murphy) for comprising the best WhatsApp group with the worst name. And finally, to my mum, dad, Stuie, Ilyse, Juliet and Asher. I'm so lucky to have you all in my life.

Oh, and I should mention my cat, Blanche DuBois, who is purring very loudly on my lap as I write this, probably as a reminder to name check her.